THE
PORNOGRAPHER'S
GRIEF

THE
PORNOGRAPHER'S
GRIEF

AND OTHER
TALES OF
HUMAN
SEXUALITY

JOSEPH GLENMULLEN, M.D.

HarperCollins*Publishers*

HarperCollins books may be purchased for educational, business, or sales promotional use. For information, please write: Special Markets Department, HarperCollins Publishers, Inc., 10 East 53rd Street, New York, NY 10022.

FIRST EDITION

Designed by Alma Hochhauser Orenstein

Library of Congress Cataloging-in-Publication Data

Glenmullen, Joseph, 1950–
    The pornographer's grief : and other tales of human sexuality / Joseph Glenmullen. — 1st ed.
        p.   cm.
    ISBN 0-06-016637-1
    1. Psychosexual disorders—Case studies. 2. Psychosexual disorders—Treatment—Case studies. 3. Psychotherapy—Case studies. I. Title.
RC556.G56   1993
616.85'83—dc20   92-53338

93 94 95 96 97 ❖/HC 10 9 8 7 6 5 4 3 2 1

To my wife,
MUIREANN

CONTENTS

ACKNOWLEDGMENTS

I cannot imagine having written this book without the encouragement and support of my friends, colleagues, mentors, students, patients, and family.

George Goethals, a senior faculty member in the Harvard University Department of Psychology and Social Relations has had a profound influence on my life, as trusted friend and mentor. He closely followed the progress of the book from its inception and provided invaluable comments as I wrote each chapter.

As a student at Harvard Medical School, I was fortunate to meet two extraordinary clinicians, Leston Havens and the late Doris Benaron. Heirs to a long tradition in psychodynamic psychiatry at Harvard, they generously shared their experience and love of psychiatric work with me.

My sincere thanks to another former teacher, Robert Coles, for generously offering to write the Foreword to the book. His scholarship and dedication to the field are exemplary.

Thanks also to Drs. Frederick Barnes, Lewis Lipsitt, and Carol Tufts, inspiring teachers during my undergraduate years at Brown University.

The steady enthusiasm displayed by my agent, Robert Lescher, has helped sustain my spirits at several critical junctures. His expertise, wisdom, and integrity have been much valued.

My editor, Hugh Van Dusen, was another early and ardent supporter. A book does not feel fully off the ground until one has an editor and publisher. I could not have asked for more in Hugh, his associate, Stephanie Gunning, and all the people at HarperCollins.

Through the years, I have had many valued colleagues in psychiatry who have helped to make the work interesting and rewarding. Especially important have been William Betcher, Barbara Burr, Win Burr, Cecilia Jones, Ellen Kane, Elissa Kleinman, and Joshua Sparrow. Special thanks also go to Randy Catlin, Chief of the Mental Health Service at the Harvard University Health Services, for his thoughtful, steady stewardship of our department.

My professional career has been enriched by teaching medical students, psychiatric residents, psychology fellows, and social work interns. Working with talented students has helped enormously to clarify my ideas and hone my skills.

I have a special gratitude for my patients, who have really taught me what I know. Their willingness to take me into their hearts and into the most intimate details of their lives has truly been a privilege.

Last, and most important, I wish to thank my wife, Muireann, to whom this book is dedicated. Our more than twenty years together nurturing family and careers have been an unending adventure and joy. She has been my source of inspiration in writing this book and in my many other endeavors.

FOREWORD

About a year before she died, I heard Anna Freud remember her father's contributions to our twentieth-century understanding of human sexuality in a manner very much like that of Dr. Glenmullen as he reflects upon his work with patients. Indeed, Miss Freud wondered what her father would make of today's social and sexual "climate" (as she put it), were he a young psychiatrist practicing "now" (she was speaking in early 1981). She spoke at some length on this matter, but the gist of her remarks, I thought, came with these comments:

> When my father first began to learn from his patients about their dreams, he had to go way beyond—he had to ignore what the outside world considered proper, and think of the patient's world. Even before he died he saw that the world had changed—sex was no longer so hidden; it was 'out in the open,' much more so than he ever dreamed would happen. People have said he was responsible—but that is not something anyone, or his ideas, can bring about. Actually, you can argue that the shifts in ways of thinking that allowed him to become so well known were the same shifts that made sexuality so public, relatively speaking. And yet ... and yet, sexuality is still a private matter, intensely so, as we know in psychoanalysis.

Even though she was nearing the end of her life, her thoughts were clear and provocative, if not stated with quite the sharpness I'd heard on previous occasions. She was anxious, really, to connect psychoanalytic interest in sexuality to the changing currents of social and cultural history. I suspect she would have admired this book on several counts: for its clarity of expression; for its careful respect for human particularity and complexity; and for its willingness to acknowledge sexual interests and expression as a major aspect of a person's life, something her father had learned gradually, and had the courage not to forget.

This book offers, really, a collection of short stories. They are stories based on clinical work, but they are presented with the novelist's sensibility—a psychiatrist's willingness to forego the professional temptations of theory, of assertive and all-too-unqualified abstraction, in favor of the subleties, ambiguities, paradoxes, and ironies that good storytelling enable. Yes, the people who appear in the following pages were patients, men and women in distress who sought out a thoughtful and compassionate doctor. But in addition to the necessary disguises to protect their privacy, these men and women have also undergone a certain kind of transfiguration—they have become characters in a series of psychological and moral fables, individuals whose fears and lusts, worries and obsessions tell us not only about themselves, but also about ourselves. We who live in late-twentieth-century, secular America so often have trouble knowing who we are, to say nothing of knowing (in the sexual sense of the word) others, even as we know so very much (through science) about the world around us, and also (through technology) how to master nature to an unprecedented degree.

Again and again, Dr. Glenmullen introduces us to a central irony of this life: Men and women who can, by and large, work well and seem in utter control of so very much, are nevertheless, with respect to intimacy, affection, and love-making, lost, confused, or terribly afraid. It has not been easy for these fellow Americans of ours—individuals of intelligence and (often enough) ambition who are (largely) successful and, by many standards, quite lucky and privileged—to come face to face with what has ailed them and why. Then there is the second, even greater, difficulty: Taking the steps to confront, head-on, their difficulties—I mean, to confront them directly themselves: their experiences, their values, their ways of seeing others, and of course, the vision they have of themselves. To quote Miss Freud again,

> After all these years, I have begun to realize that the hardest step a patient has to take—harder, even, than the work that takes place in psychoanalysis—is that first move: the decision to seek assistance, followed by the actual phone call, the actual visit to the analyst, the determination to 'see it through,' as one of my analysands put it when she was describing the various hurdles she had taken stock of, then decided to face down through analysis.

In these narratives, that determination (courage is not too strong a word here) is rewarded by the experience of conversations with a person of concentration, psychological acuity, and concern—a substantial reward, indeed. Dr. Glenmullen is too modest to say so, but I believe these stories tell us about more than human sexuality. In a larger sense, they inform us about what it is, again and again, that goes wrong in the overall life of so many men and women—a fearfulness, a learned distrust of others that ultimately expresses a worthlessness, a lesson all too many children learn at the hands of their parents well before they go to school. What helps people is not only the insight Dr. Glenmullen takes pains, every day, to offer his patients (and to us, here), but also the attitude he presents, the healing presence of someone who cares to listen, to make sense of what he has heard, to speak with candor and compassion, and thereby repairs any number of old and festering wounds. It is such an encounter in an office that benefits later encounters in bedrooms—encounters in which a heightened self-awareness and a new sense of self-respect enable the refreshing intimacy of sex to take place without the burdens, pretenses, and evasions that have previously exerted their all-too-strong influence.

In a sense, then, these are stories that belong to a literature of alienation, stories that take us into territory previously explored in fiction by John Cheever, F. Scott Fitzgerald, John Updike, Philip Roth, Mary McCarthy, and Zora Neale Hurston, to name but a few—how love, class, race, childhood experience, and family life in combination with the circumstances and the idiosyncrasies (luck, good and bad) of a particular life all conspire to make us who we are, not only in our street life, our office, factory, or shop life, and our neighborhood life, but also in our body's life, as it tries for pleasure, and in our mind's life, as it anticipates and responds to that pleasure.

ROBERT COLES, M.D.
Professor of Psychiatry and Medical Humanities
Harvard University

INTRODUCTION

I have been fortunate as a psychiatrist to have a rich and varied career. My patient population, in particular, has encompassed a wide spectrum. As is typical of many medical careers, my earliest experiences were with under-privileged patients in an urban setting, at Cambridge City and Metropolitan State hospitals, both affiliated with Harvard Medical School. First as a medical student and then as a psychiatric resident, I gravitated toward the most severely debilitated patients: chronically psychotic people on the back wards of public institutions. These schizophrenic, manic, and severely depressed individuals warmly and generously initiated me into the mysterious world of psychosis. I still treat some of these patients, and I have gone on to teach medical students, psychiatric residents, psychology fellows, and social work interns at the same institutions.

As my career developed, I began working with more fortunate people who were quite successful, often extraordinarily so. I found the lessons I learned with psychotic patients stood me well. The more capable patients could be more articulate about what troubled them, but in the end they talked about much the same things: the joys and anguish of human existence. The work with psychotic patients made me familiar with where the human psyche can go when stretched to its absolute limit. This left me both experienced and unafraid. Without hesitation, I could encourage people to wade into the depths of their pain in that cleansing ritual we call psychotherapy.

Two things in particular differentiated the work with psychotic and nonpsychotic patients. The first was the stance, or position, of the therapist. Psychotic patients are completely defenseless, vulnerable, and exquisitely sensitive to anything they perceive to be intrusive. As a therapist, a large part of my task was to help them shore up defenses to protect themselves better. At the same time, I had to be exceptionally low-key and gentle or I would scare them away, given their sensitivity and inclination to retreat psychologically. Too strong an initiative or any pressure on my part, I learned, felt crushingly intrusive to them.

By contrast, healthier, more successful patients are often too well defended. Here, the task was to help people erode defenses and discover their vulnerabilities in order to move forward in areas of their lives that were inhibited. At times, this required a very different stance: I needed to be psychologically aggressive on their behalf.

The other notable difference is how often sexual symptoms come up in the treatment. This is not to say that sexual symptoms are always present with healthier patients. Often there are no sexual difficulties at all. But it is striking how frequently sexual symptoms do arise. This was the one area I felt ill-informed about from my earlier work. How could one help somebody who had trouble reaching orgasm? What could be done about a sexual addiction? Why did the sexual symptoms seem so striking in healthier patients?

Of course, there is a rich literature on human sexuality: Freud, Ellis, Kinsey, Masters and Johnson, and Kaplan to name but a few. I read these writers, talked with colleagues, and most important, listened carefully to patients. Together we struggled with their difficulties and sorted out what helped. As always, this was an archaeological journey through the many layers of an individual's experience to discover unconscious motivations and long-forgotten influences from his or her past. In this sense, the work was no different from any other area; sexual symptoms were simply new territory. Gradually, I discerned patterns, which led to the principles and ideas in this book.

Sexuality, I began to realize, has a unique position in human existence. On the one hand, sex is a powerful, basic drive exerting tremendous influence over human behavior. On the other hand, to a surprising degree sexuality can be split off and function relatively independent of the necessities of day-to-day life. One can have an elaborate sexual problem that does not seriously affect one's ability to work and function. This can be true even if the sexual difficulty is damaging to one's self-esteem and capacity for personal relationships.

Sexual symptoms are often prominent in therapy with healthier, more successful people for this reason: Sexuality is a place where one's psychological conflicts can find ready expression, relatively cordoned off from the rest of one's life. Sexual behavior can take on unconscious, often highly complex, symbolic meaning. Indeed, human sexuality is eminently vulnerable to being put to this use. In the process, sexual behavior becomes inhibited or distorted—that is, symptomatic. Over and over again in psychotherapy one sees that sexual issues and symptoms are metaphors for the larger psychological stresses and strains in an individual's life. In hindsight, sexual problems were no doubt present in my psychotic, state-institutionalized patients, but such problems rarely came up because there were so many more pressing issues: dampening psychotic symptoms; ensuring safety; and literally securing food, clothing, and shelter.

In addition to this inherent vulnerability of sexuality, the twentieth century has been a particularly disorienting time sexually. To appreciate this, one needs to go back in history. Before the eighteenth century, sex was fairly openly integrated into everyday life. Less secrecy, reticence, and even privacy surrounded it.

This changed, quite dramatically, in the eighteenth and nineteenth centuries, which were among the most sexually repressive in Western culture. The leading historian of human sexuality, Michel Foucault, attributes the change to the industrial revolution. The growing work ethic with its emphasis on productivity and efficiency left little room for sexuality. For example, it was only in the eighteenth century that masturbation was labeled a "heinous sin of self-pollution," alleged to cause every conceivable ill, ranging from muscle weakness to insanity. While we now know such ideas to be completely unfounded, they were deeply held by medical authorities, clergy, and political leaders alike and had great influence.

In the latter half of the nineteenth century, the Victorian period capped this long, dark era of sexual repression. Relegated to the utilitarian role of procreation and robbed of pleasure, sex was shut away in the marital bedroom, codified, and shrouded in secrecy. In his book *The History of Sexuality*, Foucault says, in the shadow of the "imperial prude" grew a "restrained, mute, and hypocritical sexuality."

Not until near the end of the Victorian period, leading into the twentieth century, did a handful of European physicians begin their pioneering studies of human sexuality. Richard Krafft-Ebing began cataloging sexual perversions.

Havelock Ellis started to write openly and humanely on a wide range of sexual practices and attitudes, drawing on extensive medical and anthropological data. Sigmund Freud explored the unconscious origins of sexual and other symptoms.

On this side of the Atlantic, Margaret Mead published her influential account of the relaxed sexual coming of age of Samoans. And Alfred Kinsey conducted his exhaustive surveys of the sexual practices of Americans. As recently as the 1950s, his volume on female sexuality provoked an outraged response for reporting, among other things, that 60 percent of American women had some experience masturbating.

Slowly, these and other researchers chipped away at the Victorian facade. Meanwhile, in the field of medicine, technological advances were afoot that would radically alter the sexual landscape. The discovery of antibiotics that treated sexually transmitted diseases relieved people of this age-old scourge. Then, in 1960, oral contraceptives were introduced, allowing people unprecedented control over the other fear of sexual license: unwanted pregnancy.

Together, these social and technological developments converged in the 1960s, resulting in an explosion of sexual freedom. Every conventional standard of decorum was challenged in this tumultuous decade. All corners of society were affected, from the privacy of people's bedrooms to highly publicized lovefests to nudity on the Broadway stage. The really radical feature of the 1960s was not its rampant licentiousness, rather, it was the uncoupling of sexuality from morality. Even with the retrenchment of the 1980s, nowadays someone who is promiscuous is considered not so much immoral as perhaps ill-informed or self-destructive.

In retrospect, the freedom of the 1960s occurred in a

small, protected window in time. By the 1970s, people began to question the frequent superficiality of unchecked sexual behavior. This trend was hastened by the appearance of new, ominous, and still-incurable sexually transmitted diseases. In the 1980s the pendulum swung back in the direction of political and social conservatism. Renewed interest emerged in commitment, monogamy, and even celibacy.

This historical perspective is important because it is the context of the people and ideas described in this book. From Victorian prudery at the turn of the twentieth century, the pendulum swung to the unbridled sexual liberty of the 1960s and back again to the conservatism of the 1980s. Although these changes have been dazzling in their swiftness and breadth, all too often, in their wake, they have left people confused and conflicted. How can an individual make sense of such cultural contradictions? What standards and values can one apply toward sexuality? In addition to unconscious conflicts from one's own past, what cultural influences distort or inhibit one's sexual expression?

Such confusion and conflicts are the subject of this book. Psychiatrists have a unique view of a culture's sexual stresses and strains. Psychotherapy is one of the few places where people speak openly and honestly about their sexual behavior. The cases in this book all revolve around sexual symptoms and themes: sexual addictions, sexual dysfunctions, side effects of medications, the effects of childhood sexual trauma, and the influence of repressive religious backgrounds. Each case exemplifies a contemporary theme. Some of these are old, even ancient, ones in new guises. Others are completely new, reflecting technological advances or social change.

Naturally, I have disguised the individuals about whom I have written. To protect their privacy, their identities have been altered beyond recognition. As part of the process I informed patients and obtained their permission to use the material. To aid in camouflaging people, I have borrowed details—images, dreams, or phrases—from other patients struggling with related issues.

As written, these cases are not meant to be descriptions of the entire process of psychotherapy. Rather, the emphasis is on what might be called "psychological sleuthing," or getting to the bottom of what underlies someone's symptoms. The latter part of therapy, the slow bringing about of change, is often summarized.

While teaching psychiatry to students, I have occasionally been frustrated and have compared myself with a surgeon. A surgeon can take a medical student into the operating room and in a few hours demonstrate the peak of surgical skills, the challenges and rewards of the work. The closest approximation to this in psychiatry is called a demonstration interview: In front of an audience of students, the psychiatrist interviews a previously unknown patient. But no matter how good, one interview can never capture the highs and lows, the pathos of long-term psychotherapy. One of the many dividends of writing this book has been that, for me, it expresses some of the seemingly ineffable moments of being in psychotherapy.

THE
PORNOGRAPHER'S
GRIEF

THE PORNOGRAPHER'S GRIEF

I'm numb," said Scott.

"Numb?"

"I don't feel anything for my work or other people. I do well going about my daily business. But I feel like a zombie, an automaton, going through the motions of life."

Now in his late twenties, Scott said that this had been the case for many years.

"Look at me," he said, gesturing to his clean, wholesome look. "Bland as milk toast. And that's how I feel. Empty."

Tall, rugged, and broad shouldered, Scott was right about his conventional appearance, but his self-consciousness was a twist. Then too, at times, he had a rueful, cynical smile that gave his face more depth.

Scott, an MBA, worked for an investment firm.

"I'm an option trader," he said. "My job is to hedge, to anticipate, the market. I'm obscenely paid to be a colossal number cruncher. My work is the one thing my numbness hasn't affected."

Meanwhile, Scott said he was miserable. People liked and respected him at work. He socialized and had friends. But he felt distant and removed from others, always an outsider. Scott thought other people did not know the degree to which he felt estranged. Even in sports, which he played avidly, he felt he was "bouncing off people" rather than being passionately involved.

"Are you in a relationship?" I asked.

"For the past four years," Scott replied self-consciously. "I imagine that sounds contradictory. But there, too, I'm going through the motions."

"For four years?"

"I suppose I do love her." Scott waffled, demonstrating his confusion in the emotional realm. "But I can't feel it. I can't make a commitment to her. The relationship, the way it's stagnating, is a big part of why I'm getting into therapy."

Scott said he and his girlfriend, Elizabeth, met socially about a year before they began dating. The relationship had been exclusive for the past four years. The couple once entertained the possibility of living together but never did because the relationship had not progressed to that point. Scott commented that one of the manifestations of his stagnation and lack of commitment was that some time ago he had withdrawn sexually from Elizabeth. "I'm lukewarm, indifferent to sex with her," he disclosed.

Scott felt guilty about this. Withdrawing sexually from women had been a pattern in his relationships. This would start to happen after the early courting phase was over. Given Scott's numbness generally, I wondered if he had any form of strong sexual drive and asked, "Do you have other sexual outlets?"

"Well, yes . . . I masturbate." Scott blushed. "I feel guilty doing that while in a relationship."

"I see."

"I'm pretty puritanical," Scott continued. "From Bible country, you know. I find sex difficult to talk about."

Scott's chief symptom, his numbness, is an increasingly

common one, especially among men. In my experience, the numbness is usually a response to some insufferable pain. Established over many years, it can take considerable time to reverse.

Curious about his history, I asked Scott in a later session to tell me about his background. The first words out of his mouth were that he had a "somewhat unusual childhood." This was a considerable understatement given what was to follow.

Scott grew up in Nebraska. His parents had a very difficult marriage. His father, who referred to himself as an entrepreneur, was in fact "something of a con artist." He was in and out of an endless stream of businesses and get-rich-quick schemes that turned out to be scams. Scott said the family was constantly being driven out of town over his father's latest enterprise. As a result, the family moved every few years. Scott's mother was always patient and enduring. There would be brief periods in which it had extra money, but most of the time, the family scraped by.

Then, when Scott was fourteen years old, his father disappeared. He recalled vividly the day this occurred. "I came down one morning dressed for school, and my mother was sitting at the kitchen table crying. 'Your father never came home last night,' she said. She knew something serious was wrong. For all his difficulties, my father never stayed away from home. Home was where he always took refuge. My mother called the police but they more or less laughed at her. They thought it was just one more man out all night with his buddies or another woman. But I knew she was right. Walking to school that morning I was afraid life would never be the same."

Scott said his mother "pretty much had a nervous breakdown." He never knew the details, but she quickly discovered a new financial scandal, much worse and more embarrassing than the others. Her frantic efforts to find the father were fruitless. For the first time in her life, she had to go to work to support Scott and his brother and sister. After all his mother had been through with the father, standing by him, always moving, she never expected to be abandoned. She was openly angry, bitter, and resentful.

For his part, Scott was confused and hurt. He had always liked his father, who was "charismatic" and "great with kids." Scott said his father had never followed through with things, but this had not mattered because his mother usually picked up the pieces. Scott spent the months immediately after his father disappeared "kicking around the yard," dejected and sad.

As is usually the case, the family experienced a drastic change in financial circumstances, and the situation became much worse than it had ever been. A month after his father disappeared, most of the furniture in the house was repossessed. Scott recalled that day after day he hoped his father would come back so things would return to normal.

About six months after he disappeared, the father was found dead in a hotel room. Only when he told me this did Scott flinch, betraying the slightest hint of emotion. He said it was never clear whether his father committed suicide or was killed by people he cheated or to whom he owed money. Scott's mother's anger turned to grief, which she "never recovered from."

Scott's junior high and high school years were "the worst." His mother went to work as a secretary in a factory, but it took her years to reach a position of modest responsibility and remuneration. She barely managed to hold on to the family home, and for years they were "pretty destitute."

At the end of the session, I asked Scott what feelings he had telling me all this.

"None. It's like I'm describing someone else's life, or a movie. That's the problem."

I understood much better why Scott was so numb. Obviously, he had had a devastating loss. The loss was compounded by the fact that his mother, too, was depressed and overwhelmed. Under the circumstances, she no doubt was unable to attend to his grief. With no place to take his feelings, they became stifled. Eventually, Scott reached the state of generalized numbness that now troubled him.

The greatest challenge to such numbness is a new intimate relationship. Intimate relationships demand strong feelings and stir up old ones. Scott was four years into a relationship he was quite confused about. People with losses like Scott's often have trouble with depth and commitment in relationships. On the one hand, they cannot be without the security of a relationship. On the other hand, they are terrified of letting go, of giving heart and soul, because of their chilling experience.

Scott's numbness was indeed quite severe. He had a straight-arrow, virtually emotionless, quality. In the ensuing months, I went into some depth with him about the difficult junior high and high school years. Scott described a stoic self-sufficiency in coping with his new circumstances. His family, including his father, had long been involved in a fundamentalist Christian church. When his father disappeared, Scott's mother experienced a new religious zeal. The church became her principal source of emotional support. Materially, too, the church tried to help out with clothes and food.

"For the first few years, people from the church would arrive on Christmas Eve with gifts, and those were the only gifts we received," said Scott. "I hated their gifts."

"Why did you hate them?"

"The do-gooders. . . . I didn't want their pity."

Scott said this so flatly one could have missed its powerful emotional content. I imagined the young boy who felt spurned and bitter. Here already was the outsider, unable to embrace the community support his mother so desperately needed. Perhaps there was some condescension which Scott sensed on the part of the alms givers. In any case, here he was at a young age cynical and rejecting. One could only imagine his burning resentment and sense of isolation in those Christmas Eve scenes.

I commented to this effect to Scott, but at this stage in our work it went past him. Still, this was an important role of mine in the therapy: to articulate the repressed emotions, to resonate with the stifled part of Scott, to re-create and legitimize the emotional field. I could not be entirely accurate imagining what Scott felt but a reasonable inference would more than suffice to jog him.

Commenting further on the family's religion, Scott described the sect as fire and brimstone: dry, humorless, and severe. Emotions and sexuality "had no place."

"That is, except emotions for God," he said. "I don't know if you've ever seen a fundamentalist minister preach, but there's a fevered pitch and almost veiled sexuality to it. They're usually reasonably good-looking young men who cavort across the front of the church as though onstage. Sometimes they're even gripping a microphone if the congregation is big enough to warrant amplification."

Scott said he was encouraged to surrender his grief to God. "I think that's where the pattern of my denial began. It's not the same thing as true grieving. It's a kind of perverted abdication of emotions."

Later on, in college, Scott had to overcome considerable

sexual inhibitions because of his religious background. He noted, "I wasn't even used to touching, let alone kissing and sexual intimacy. I'm still somewhat mechanical and uptight. I know my sexual withdrawal from Elizabeth and earlier girlfriends is connected to repressed feelings and anguish about my father."

For some time Scott and I progressed in this way, building a fledgling vocabulary of feelings for his experience. Then, around four months into the therapy, Scott began to draw back. It was as though unconsciously he felt he had already told me too much. Even the primitive level of emotion we had reached was overwhelming. Slowly, he narrowed the focus of our discussions: In each meeting he told me one or two overdetailed stories, descriptions of his interactions with people during the week, which were examples of his numbness. I listened patiently to these accounts, although they added little to the picture.

Eventually, Scott talked about his numbness to the exclusion of all else. The effect on our work was deadening. I tried unsuccessfully to divert him back to the subject of his father, his history, or some other less narrowly focused area. As he recounted one tedious report after another, Scott's early image of himself as a titanic number cruncher loomed large. Paying attention and following his minutiae began to require effort.

This can be a dangerous time in a psychotherapy. The risk is that out of boredom and frustration the therapist will subtly reject or, worse, lash out at the patient in a harmful way. I consoled myself that Scott needed this reprieve, however oppressive. Endurance and patience were required on my part. All the while I sat wondering, How, with this man, will I get back to some emotion?

* * *

Months later, a surprising revelation took the therapy in a new direction. While he continued doggedly to give detailed descriptions of his numbness, Scott began to complain it was not getting any better. He speculated he might be a "hopeless case." He berated himself for this, but scrupulously avoided any criticism of the therapy or me. Often people who have difficulty with emotions will be unaware of, or hesitant to express, anger toward the therapy. Knowing this, I attempted to provide Scott with an opportunity to express any feelings that might be there. So desolate was the emotional field that even umbrage would be welcome.

One day I said, "Perhaps you're disappointed things haven't changed faster since you've been seeing me."

"No," Scott insisted. "It's my fault I'm not making any progress." After some further discussion, he added, "I just can't help thinking a lot of the time that I must be a very frustrating patient for you."

A disclaimer such as this can be evidence of unconscious passive-aggressive feelings. Wanting to seize any opportunity to stir up emotion, I said provocatively, "I wonder if that's what you want to be?"

Scott looked dismayed.

Over the next few weeks Scott's discontent escalated. I considered this a good sign; the emotional tone of our meetings was rising. Then, in a decisive session, Scott revealed for the first time that he took late-night walks and complained that they were occurring with increasing frequency. He typically left home after midnight and would be gone close to an hour, "pounding the pavement."

"Where do you go?" I asked, surprised.

"I walk around the city. I observe the people one sees out at that hour: lowlife, night life."

"What motivates you to take the walks?"

"I don't know. I'm telling you because I think they're dangerous."

"You feel they're dangerous but go anyway?"

"I can't resist. It's a kind of urge," said Scott. "I've done this on and off for years but in the last few months it's gotten worse."

"The last few months meaning the time you've been seeing me?"

Scott looked embarrassed but said yes.

"You walk around. You observe the night life. And then go home?"

"Right."

"What do you do when you get home?"

"I go to bed."

"Immediately?"

"I'm usually exhausted. I . . . read for a while and then fall asleep."

"That's all?"

Clearly embarrassed, Scott added, "First I . . . I jerk off. Then I fall asleep."

I had begun to suspect a sexual overtone to Scott's walks.

"Does anything else happen on the walks?"

"No," he answered defensively.

"You don't meet anyone?"

"Like who?"

"You don't pick someone up or get picked up?"

"No!" Scott responded angrily. "You should know I'm not capable of that."

"What is it you read before jerking off and falling asleep?"

"I don't want to go into it."

"Something you buy on the walks?"

Scott shook his head nervously.

"Pornography?"

"How did you know?" Scott appeared stunned.

"You mentioned an uncontrollable urge and a compulsion to take walks. When a sexual connection emerged, there weren't many possibilities."

Scott sat frozen in his chair for some time. At first he looked petrified but gradually eased. Eventually, he said, "I can't believe the secret's out . . . after all these years."

"How do you feel?"

"Embarrassed. Ashamed."

This was not a surprise. Many men who compulsively buy pornography feel this way. Had he felt differently, Scott would have told me long ago.

"I suppose," he added, "I feel some relief."

"Can you say more about the relief?"

"For years I've been so ashamed and secretive about my habit. But I think part of me has wanted to tell someone for a long time."

"I imagine that's true," I said supportively.

Indeed, now I had a whole new slant on Scott's narrow focus on his numbness, his awkwardness in the therapy and his slight hostility: All the while he was sitting on a secret he felt conflicted about telling me.

"I buy pornographic magazines and take them home," Scott said, looking a little more relaxed.

"Videos too?"

"Rarely. The television's in the living room, and because of my roommates it's not easy."

"I see."

With a guilty look, Scott elaborated. "After the walks, when I get home with the magazines, I have an orgy."

"An orgy?"

"The excitement of getting the pornography brings something out in me, some animal. It's awful."

We were at the close of the session, and in conclusion, I said, "It isn't awful. Quite the contrary, it's good."

"Good?" Scott expressed surprise.

"Not the pornography. It's too bad you need the pornography to access your vitality. But the good news is you're not as numb as you've been saying. You're not so dead. You have a secret life, between midnight and two in the morning, on a regular basis when you're unhinged with emotion and sexuality."

Scott's disclosure felt like a missing link falling into place: He was not simply an automaton. Here was a human frailty, an irresistible urge. How could anyone have been as lifeless as he alleged? He made much more sense now, even though his impulse raised more questions than it answered.

The discovery of Scott's furtive sexual life revitalized the therapy. In subsequent weeks and months, we discussed his disclosure in detail. He described a compulsion that would unexpectedly overcome him. The compulsion might not occur for weeks, during which time Scott would "forget" his "dirty habit." At other times the need to acquire pornography would occur almost daily. Once the idea came over him, he was unable to resist. He said, "My heart starts to pound and I know sooner or later I'm going to do it. I hate it. It's so disruptive of my normal routines. Sometimes I've had to decline to see or stay with Elizabeth because I knew I had to do this."

Late at night, en route to a store, Scott would experience a nervous anticipation. "Usually I just go to news agents and convenience stores," he said. "But occasionally I journey into the 'Combat Zone' [Boston's red-light district]. I often feel like a sexual Jekyll and Hyde: By day I move in the most conservative, staid of circles. By night I traffic in the city's underside. I'm always terrified of encountering someone I know."

"Has that happened?"

"Occasionally, I'll see someone I recognize. Once I bumped into a client. That was awful."

"What did you do?"

"We said nothing to one another, and it was never mentioned."

Because he feared being seen, Scott never bought magazines near where he lived.

"I always walk somewhere that's half an hour or more away. I walk briskly, and by the time I get to a store I'm exhausted but kind of high."

Scott described the scenes he typically passed en route: neon signs, sidewalk litter, street people bundled up in doorways for the night, policemen, cabbies, drug dealers, and people he imagined were pimps with their prostitutes. He described these scenes in a more gripping way than usual. I thought these walks were rituals for Scott: This was a highly constricted man descending into his sexuality.

Once at a newsstand or store, there were two salient features for Scott in purchasing pornography. The first was the other customers. "I'm acutely aware of other men perusing the magazines. There's no verbal communication but it's like you're jointly involved in something taboo. I sometimes wonder what turns another man on. Occasionally I'll pick up a magazine just as someone else has put it down, so there's a kind of . . . "

"A kind of what?"

"I don't know. The magazine is still warm with his

touch when I lift it . . . there's a connection, oddly, of some sort."

The other striking feature of Scott's experience was going to the cash register and paying for his magazines. "I'm always intrigued by that exchange," he said. "You have to hand the magazines to this stranger who rings them up, takes your money, and gives you back the goods."

"What intrigues you?"

"This is someone who knows what you're doing. I always wonder what they think."

"What do you imagine they think?" I asked.

"Do they disapprove? Do they think I'm a pervert?" Scott answered.

I thought this was a projective test: What Scott imagined went on in the other person's head was an indication of how he himself felt.

"Then again," he continued, "another part of me feels like 'Fuck you' toward the person if they are being judgmental. You're every bit as bad, I think. You're colluding with me. You're profiting from it, which is worse."

Here was the bitter, cynical side of Scott. What did he imagine I thought of him? What might he think unconsciously about my profiting from hearing him describe his affliction?

"Of course, the whole thing is ridiculous on my part. Most of the people in those jobs are semicomatose. They don't appear to have a thought in their heads as customers come and go."

"Is the experience any different for you if it's a man or a woman?"

"Behind the counter?"

I nodded.

"I don't think so. Perhaps I feel a little more comfortable if it's a man; a little more guilty if it's a woman. I don't understand how women can work in that kind of environment."

I asked Scott what kind of magazines he bought. Given the limitless possibilities, his preferences would indicate something about the underlying emotions and sexual issues he was acting out through the pornography.

"What do you mean?" he asked.

"There are lots of different kinds: straight, gay, soft porn, hard porn, people alone or in groups."

"I only ever buy soft porn," Scott was quick to respond. "I have enough conflicts buying it. I don't go near the violent, hard stuff. In fact, I find it revolting." After a brief pause, he added, "And I only buy heterosexual magazines. Homosexual material turns me off."

"Do you have any favorite, prototypic scenes?"

Scott was circumspect. "No. Not really."

I thought he might be hedging. "Nothing comes to mind?"

"No." Scott shook his head.

Once he purchased the magazines, Scott would go straight home. In the privacy of his room he would spend anywhere from fifteen minutes to hours stimulating himself sexually and eventually reaching orgasm. As it is for most people, masturbation was the eventual goal of buying pornography.

"I detest the amount of time and money I spend on this," Scott said angrily. "The magazines are expensive and I buy two or three at a time. I keep having to throw them away because I wouldn't want anyone to ever find them. Besides, old magazines don't excite me; I have to buy new ones to be aroused. Can you imagine the time spent going and coming from a store? An hour on average! Plus another hour jerking off."

Scott's arguments sounded like rationalizations. The cost could hardly be a hardship for him. Old magazines need not be so ineffectual. I thought Scott kept buying new ones in order to take the ritual walks. I suspected these were at least as important to him as the magazines themselves.

Because most people prolong masturbation to enhance the experience, I was surprised when Scott said, "I hold out as long as I can because I know I'm going to feel so terrible."

"Terrible? You don't have a sense of relief or pleasure?"

"Relief only in a physical sense," Scott said bitterly. "That's all. Certainly not pleasure. I come because I have to, to get it over with. But what I feel at that moment is shame and guilt for not being able to control my impulses, for having failed once again."

I thought this too self-depriving. Why was Scott loath to admit sexual pleasure to himself? Where did so much guilt come from? Was there more to it than just guilt?

Scott's compulsion to buy pornography was an addiction. The concept of sexual addiction is a relatively new one that is rapidly gaining credibility. Like other addictions, sexual ones begin with an irresistible urge. This is followed by a procurement ritual, an adrenaline-high state in which the individual follows an established set of steps to obtain a fix. The result is some form of climax, satiety, and calm. In the future, the cycle invariably begins again.

As we discussed Scott's fixation, he said it became worse. He was distressed by this; I was relatively unperturbed. For all its problems, this impulse, for now, had a franchise on his emotional life. I was not surprised it could become worse before getting better. His divulging and discussing it with me was surely stirring a lot up.

Talking about his addiction, Scott began to debate whether or not to confide in Elizabeth. "I feel badly that someone else knows and she doesn't. When it was a complete secret, I felt differently."

Scott said the duplicity of his activity increasingly bothered him. He would like to be honest with Elizabeth. He might need her help in order to change.

I thought these were good sentiments. Presumably, they indicated a change in Scott, a new openness. His feelings also bespoke a considerable degree of involvement and depth with Elizabeth.

One morning, Scott called unexpectedly to request an extra appointment. When I saw him later in the day he said he was in a crisis.

"I told Elizabeth!" he proceeded to blurt out.

"About the pornography?"

"Yes. She's quite upset. She's beside herself in fact."

"What exactly did she say?"

"She was shocked. It wasn't just the magazines that bothered her, although she certainly doesn't like pornography. She was also upset about the parts of town I sometimes go into . . . the secrecy . . . the idea I've had this other life that excluded her."

Elizabeth was up all night after Scott's revelation and could not go to work. In fact, he stayed home with her.

"How is she doing now?" I asked.

"As a matter of fact, she's in the waiting room," Scott announced. "We didn't know whether or not you'd want to see her."

This was interesting phraseology, I thought.

"Would she like to see me?"

"I think so," Scott said sheepishly.

"How do you feel about it?"

"I'd like that too."

"Why don't you bring her in."

Scott was attentive in introducing Elizabeth. She was his equal in her wholesome appearance. I could see instantly why Scott's revelation had been difficult for her. However, she was a solid-looking person who, I thought, probably would weather this and be an asset to Scott in his struggles.

"We have been talking for a while about Scott's compulsion to buy pornography," I said to Elizabeth when the couple were seated. "I gather he told you last night and it's been hard to take."

Elizabeth nodded.

"It would be helpful if you could tell me in your own words how you're feeling."

I had not noticed before that Elizabeth was holding a soggy mass of tissues in her hand. Touching them to her face, she began crying and said, "Scott and I have been going out for four years. We've had a lot of trouble because he couldn't make a commitment. That was bad enough. I had no idea this was going on on the side."

Despite her distress, Elizabeth was quite articulate on the subject of the pornography. She now thought she "did not know" Scott. How could he have led this clandestine life all these years?

"He told me," she said haltingly, "there were times when he made excuses to me that he was too tired to come over or go out, then went and did this. He knew he was going to do it! He lied to me." Elizabeth's face darkened, her mouth quivered, and she looked accusingly at Scott. "He's had sex with dirty magazines when he wouldn't have sex with me."

White as a sheet, Scott apologized profusely.

For Elizabeth, the biggest issue was feeling rejected. "Why does he need these magazines? Why does he prefer them to me? I must not satisfy him. I mustn't be what he wants."

"That's not true," Scott said, anguished. "It has nothing to do with you."

"How can it have nothing to do with me?"

"It has nothing to do with my feelings or attraction for you."

"I told him last night," Elizabeth said assertively, "to ravish me. 'If you want to do perverse things, do them with me. Don't resort to these sleaze-ball places and filthy magazines.'"

Elizabeth's lack of squeamishness was reassuring. However, a little while later she was vengeful. "Has he told you he's an uptight prick in bed? He hasn't the guts to experiment in the flesh."

Elizabeth was clearly feeling wounded and angry. The couple's pain and the gap between Elizabeth and Scott were evident. Nevertheless, they were making a valiant effort to communicate.

Particularly in a crisis such as this, one often finds oneself interpreting for the patient to the partner or spouse. Naturally, Scott's revelation was a shock, I said to Elizabeth. Her agitated reaction was completely understandable. How could she feel otherwise?

Then I responded to her three concerns, addressing them in a way that Scott had been unable to. First, in regard to "not knowing him," I said I thought Scott did not know large parts of himself. That was why he came to therapy, largely at Elizabeth's urging. We were working on the problem but still had a long way to go. I thought Scott's pornography addiction was somehow related to his emotional constriction. As yet, I could not be any more articulate than this but imagined the pornography was a symptom of something larger.

Scott nodded, indicating I was on the mark.

Second, I said, as best she could, it would be better if Elizabeth did not take Scott's addiction personally. I knew this was difficult to do. Indeed, it was probably impossible to do completely. But Scott's habit predated his relationship with her by a long time. I suspected he was right in saying it had little to do with her. I thought dissatisfaction with Elizabeth or hostility toward women in general was unlikely to be Scott's underlying problem.

Third, and more speculative, I thought Scott's addiction was related to a point of fairly low self-esteem. I was concerned Elizabeth's vehement disapproval might, in fact, be what he was looking for. There was self-loathing in what he did, and he expected others to mirror it.

"He may even have told you of his addiction at this particular point in time," I suggested, "because he did not get this reaction from me. While consciously he doesn't want to be judged, I think unconsciously he's looking for disapproval. When he didn't get it here, he may have turned to you."

Scott protested, but Elizabeth was intrigued by this possibility. I told her I thought it would be unproductive for her to get caught up in a vicious circle condemning him.

"Does that mean I have to think what he does is wonderful?" Elizabeth asked a little sarcastically.

"That wouldn't even be helpful. I think your stand is clear to Scott. But he needs some space."

In the end, the couple was more relaxed and thanked me

for meeting with them. Seeing Elizabeth was helpful for me too. I now knew Scott's partner. For the next few weeks he kept me informed of their ongoing discussions. One day, about a month after I saw them together, he began, mirthfully, "You know what Elizabeth did?"

"No. What?"

"First she went and bought some women's pornographic magazines. You know, with pictures of men in them. She wanted me to wear the other shoe. I have to admit I felt a twinge of jealousy."

I was impressed with Elizabeth's tactics.

"But she later confessed the magazines didn't do much for her. She can't understand why anyone would buy them repeatedly. Then she did something much bigger. . . . I think it's okay to tell you. She didn't say not to." Here Scott broke into an embarrassed smile. "She presented me with some pinups of herself."

"Pinups of herself?"

"I guess she had the pictures taken a couple of weeks ago. She got a friend to photograph her naked in a few positions. She said it was difficult to overcome her modesty. The woman enlarged the pictures to centerfold size. Elizabeth gave them to me and said, 'If you need to look at pictures, look at mine.'"

I found this endearing, further evidence of Elizabeth's ingenuity and strength. Months later, I looked back on this nostalgically: If only such a playful maneuver could have been a cure. Unfortunately, we all had to wait patiently through another long phase in which Scott made little progress with his addiction.

Addictions almost always wax and wane. Only when an addiction is life threatening does one have a chance of convincing someone to bring it to an abrupt halt. As Scott's therapy progressed, we returned to the subjects of his childhood: the death of his father, his adolescence and sexuality, and his conservative religious background. Since telling me about his sexual compulsion, he was generally much more open. However, he was still quite limited emotionally.

After many months of such discussion, a new avenue finally emerged. One day, while discussing sexuality, Scott said he never masturbated without pornography!

"You don't ever have your own sexual fantasies?" I asked, surprised.

Scott shook his head. "No. Never."

"What about sexual dreams?"

"I don't have sexual dreams."

Initially, I was skeptical, but I became convinced, and have since seen this in other men with pornography addictions. Here was new evidence that the addiction was a proxy for Scott's emotional life: The pornography filled a void, a lack of spontaneity on his part. As we talked, he referred to the sexual scenes as "out there," "on the page," "someone else's invention." Gradually, I began to suspect the pornography served yet another role: It not only filled a void but, more important, was a defense against Scott's own inner life. The "out there on the page" meant it was not his. When I broached this with Scott, he said, "Well, yes. Then I'm not responsible for it."

Only then did I begin lobbying Scott to resist the pornographic temptation. I explained that as long as the pornography was in place, I thought he would be blocked from connecting with large pieces of his emotional life, imagination, and sexuality.

Scott was disturbed by the idea that the pornography was a defense. However, he was ambivalent about change.

He vacillated between efforts to curtail his activity and rationalizations to maintain it. He was surprised and embarrassed by how difficult it was to initiate restraint. When he failed, which he did repeatedly, he fell back on doubts: Why was it necessary to have one's own fantasy life? What was wrong with purchasing the sexual fantasies of others?

In the past, Scott explained, weeks would sometimes go by in which he "forgot" about buying pornography. Now, making a self-conscious effort to stop, he was unable to go more than a few days without succumbing to the habit. Scott was almost tearful as he told me. Regardless of one's moral or political stance on pornography, at such close range one could not help feeling compassionate toward Scott, seeing how much he was suffering.

One week, agitated and distressed, he launched into an anguished soliloquy. "I'm not hurting anyone with what I do. I suppose one could argue the women, and men, are being used. They're being objectified in the process. I've heard they're paid next to nothing for posing. But I'm being used too. I can't help myself. I feel terrible about what I do. I don't buy anything with violence in it. What I like is quite benign, relatively speaking. It's just exhibitionism: people showing off great bodies and others getting their rocks off on it."

When Scott quieted, I said sympathetically, "If you don't want to change you don't have to, but I still think you're frustrated with the status quo."

Becoming defensive, Scott insisted sexual fantasies were "bad."

"They're far better than pornography," I replied.

"You're judging me for the pornography," Scott retorted, extremely sensitive on this point.

"I didn't say that. I said your own fantasies would be

preferable." In fact, I had scrupulously avoided any judgmental stance. Scott felt loathsome enough about his activity. Any hint of judgment on my part could rupture the therapy.

Scott again attributed his intense sexual conflicts to his religious background. I said the religion was certainly an influence, but I now thought the bigger issue was distance from his own inner life. To allow himself free reign in fantasy would run counter to his emotional restraint.

Looking once more for hints of what the pornography expressed, I asked Scott again if there was any prototypic scenes he gravitated to.

"I've thought about that since you asked," said Scott. "It's certainly true when I'm browsing through magazines I'm looking for things that turn me on. Most of what you see is reclining nude bodies, a woman filling a page. That certainly turns me on. But if I'm honest about what's my favorite, it's . . . threesomes."

"With?"

"Two men and a woman."

"What is it you like about such a group?"

"I have no idea. It's just very arousing to me."

"Can you say anything more? Any activities or positions you especially like? What you imagine the relationship between the people is?"

"Not really. Mm . . . that they're friends."

"Friends?"

"The two men are somehow friends. It's not competitive. But that's all. I can't think of anything else."

We again hit the limit of what Scott could articulate. Still, his interest in the threesomes was telling. Something about his addiction had to do with Scott's relationship to men, I thought. I recalled his awareness of the other men in a shop when he was looking through magazines. It struck me the world of pornography, like some pool halls and bars and certain sports, is very much a world of men.

Eventually, Scott began to put together weeks of abstinence. Like many people early in sobriety, the first thing he noticed was that he was much more emotional. For example, during one of these periods Scott had an unusual experience at work. One of his bosses, a managing director in the firm, was critical of something Scott did. At first, Scott was politic, responding in his usual style. Then, out of the blue, he burst into tears. Scott said this was embarrassing both for him and for the other man, who was quite incompetent emotionally and felt at a complete loss.

I asked Scott in detail what he had done wrong, what the nature of the criticism was, exactly what was said, how it was delivered, and about his relationship to the man. I was looking for what particularly had upset him. As he told the story, it appeared he was paying less attention to details at work. This was not surprising given how much was going on in the rest of his life.

The most salient feature, however, was that the man was someone whose opinion Scott cared a lot about, a much older man whom Scott respected and looked up to. He was crushed by the criticism. My thought was that this man was a father figure. The whole episode, breaking down, was extremely uncharacteristic of Scott and disturbing to him.

Sometimes when one has laid all the groundwork in therapy, one is not even aware of it. You do not realize the barrier between the patient and their walled off emotions has been worn down to a thin membrane until, unsuspectingly, you ask a question that pierces the membrane, and together you and the patient suddenly fall headlong into the heretofore unreachable abyss.

During one of his sober, more emotionally vulnerable weeks, I asked about Scott's earliest experiences with pornography, when and where he first bought it.

To my dismay, Scott turned crimson and averted his face. Tears began streaming down his cheeks before he answered. "I didn't buy it. I found it on a bookshelf in my father's study."

"The pornography is a connection to him."

"I used to be so embarrassed about the pornography. . . . I'm even more embarrassed to have gotten it from him."

"How old were you?"

"Thirteen maybe. About a year before he left."

"And you found it in his study?"

"Sandwiched in between some otherwise innocuous books. Not hidden very well actually, since I found it. He had a folder with a few magazines and lots of pictures, centerfolds he'd torn out of other magazines he must have thrown away. I guess he didn't want to keep too big a stash."

"Would you go to the study often?"

Scott nodded. "I borrowed the magazines to masturbate. It weirded me out a little to think the same pictures turned my father on."

"Did he ever find out you used them?"

"I don't think so."

"How would he have reconciled this with his religiosity?"

"How did he reconcile anything?" Scott responded sardonically.

I thought of his entrepreneur father, the charismatic confidence man, the Bible-thumping fundamentalist with pornography, who had disappeared.

Scott continued, "What I always wondered was, Did my

mother know? Did she ever find out? If so, what did she think of us?"

I noted Scott's use of the word *us,* the secret father-son pair.

"When he left, did you keep the folder?"

"It was gone."

"Gone?"

"He must have cleaned it out with other things he didn't want people to find."

"Is that when you began buying magazines?"

"At fourteen? In a small town? I couldn't have gotten near them."

"So you went without for a number of years?"

"No."

"What did you do?"

"Remember I told you about kicking around the yard in the months after he disappeared?"

"Yes."

"I don't know exactly when it began, but a short while later I started taking long bike rides, to get away. I bicycled miles in the flat countryside, corn country, and made a curious discovery: Along the heavily traveled arteries I found magazines . . . tossed out of car windows into the low grass by the roadside."

My face registered the significance of this extraordinary image.

"It makes sense," Scott explained. "Men buy magazines. I guess they look at them in their cars but don't want to take them home. So, when they're finished, they toss them out the window. I found all kinds of pornography in various stages of decay. Garbage actually but where else could a young boy come by it. It was another world. I discovered it fortuitously really."

"A world of men."

"Right."

"A mysterious connection . . . "

Scott nodded.

". . . to your father."

"I'd forgotten all this until recently it came back to me. It's a long time since I've thought of it like that."

"Well, later in your life it's transformed. The connection's no longer obvious."

"How do you mean?"

"I have this image of you as a boy, sad and lonely, bicycling to get away. At the same time perhaps the treks vaguely served the purpose of looking for your father."

Scott nodded in agreement.

"You didn't find him, but you stumbled on this curious tie to him. Later, when you get to the city, it's very different. The bicycle is gone. The cornfields are gone. Your home is gone. You're just another man procuring pornographic magazines in urban shops. The relation to your father is obscured. All that's left are the walks. . . ."

"The walks?" Scott interjected.

"I think they replaced the bike rides."

"I see."

"Then there's your awareness of the other men in a shop, the feeling you're doing something together that is taboo. The vague sense of connection you feel picking up a magazine still warm with another man's touch. But that's all that's left. The tie with your father is no longer obvious. It's become symbolic, transformed and obscured."

The evocative imagery brought Scott home. For a long time he sat crying, his face raw with emotion. He kept putting his hand up to his forehead, as though he were trying to press on the excruciating pain.

* * *

The remainder of Scott's therapy was what is referred to as grief work. Even when it only finds expression years after the loss, grief follows a fairly characteristic course. Moving into the depths of his sadness, Scott expressed a secret fear it was his fault his father left. Children with a loss like Scott's nearly always feel this way. Rational arguments alter this position only slowly. Even knowing the circumstances under which his father disappeared, Scott asked with anguish, "How could I not have mattered enough for him to stay?"

Anger is always the most difficult emotion in grief. A very natural emotion, people do not expect it and think it is bad, or wrong. Anger is the most common reason why grief is unresolved. Scott spent months on his anger at having been abandoned. He was convinced his father left of his own volition. "He took the folder . . . ," Scott said, referring back to the pornography, with its central position. "He had time to pack it and a lot of other things. Even if he'd gone to jail for a while, we could have had a relationship."

Scott went over in new detail the years immediately after his father left. Initially, he did not want other children at school to know. He would lie, saying his father was away on business.

"For all I knew, it was true," Scott rationalized.

Reality became impossible to deny when his father was found dead. Scott described a dramatic change in himself from a fairly outgoing, sociable child to a withdrawn, lonely one.

As part of his grieving, Scott talked with his brother and sister. They related their own difficulties coming to terms with their father's death. They believed their mother would still be unable to deal with the issue.

Elizabeth was very supportive of Scott. She accompanied him to therapy on several occasions. While sympathetic to his situation, she was also relieved to have an explanation for his addiction.

Stripped of its purpose, Scott's pornography addiction gradually fell away. Eventually, he had pornographic urges only rarely, at times of high stress, which is to be expected in someone with a former addiction.

As in Scott's case, many addictions are identifications with a parent. This is true not only of sexual addictions but also of alcoholism and other drug dependencies. Ironically, the identification is usually with a parent with whom the child had a difficult or distant relationship.

Scott was an extreme case in that his father had disappeared and died. However, in other young men with pornography addictions, I have often seen a similar pattern. That is, the addiction is an identification with a distant father that began with discovering pornography while rooting among the father's possessions.

THE WOMAN WHO THOUGHT HER ORGASM WAS A GIFT

It is surprising how often sex is a metaphor for the larger issues troubling a relationship. But this may not be apparent early on in a psychotherapy, because people are often cautious when it comes to talking about the most intimate details of their sexual life. Especially when sexual dysfunction is present, they may be embarrassed or ashamed. Also, they may mistakenly think no help is available for these problems. And so the sexual dysfunction is hidden or covered up, usually not by outright lies but by misleading answers to questions that are too general. Only later on, when trust and confidence in the therapy have been established, does the sexual dysfunction emerge, often accidentally, contradicting statements made earlier on.

Such was the case with Anne and Jonathan, a couple in their twenties who came to see me with concerns about their relationship. From the first they struck me as a curious match. As I entered the waiting room to collect them for our initial meeting, Anne came forward immediately to introduce herself. She was a tall, outgoing woman, fashionably dressed in a pale, well-cut business suit. She had a lively, pleasant smile and held one's gaze as she spoke. After introducing herself, she turned to Jonathan. By contrast, he had a sultry, artsy look. A thin young man, he was dressed in jeans and an oversize sports jacket. He had stayed back at some distance and only now came forward. Was it a wary look that crossed his face as we shook hands?

Inside my office, Anne took the lead in explaining why they had come. Jonathan spoke mostly to correct her, to fix a date a little more precisely or to disagree on a detail. Recent college graduates, they had been living together in Boston for two years. In the previous twelve months, their relationship had deteriorated seriously. What little time they spent together was marred by bitter, sarcastic fighting. Most recently the fighting had taken on a particularly acrimonious tone, which is why they came to therapy. As is typically the case, the idea for couples therapy had come from the female partner. Jonathan had reluctantly come along.

Indeed, as our meeting progressed things rapidly deteriorated between them. His corrections became increasingly hostile. Her narrative grew more strident. Anne believed the problems in their relationship were due to Jonathan's "overcommitment" to work.

"I am not overcommitted," he said angrily.

Jonathan was in the technical, computer end of the motion picture industry, Anne explained, and his work took him to New York City much of the time. His frequent travel upset her. She insisted he was using his work to avoid the relationship. After moving in together, she maintained, he abandoned her for his computers and work. She alleged he did not need to spend as much time in New York as he did.

"You've created a virtual long-distance relationship," she accused him.

"It's not my fault we live in Boston," Jonathan hurled back. "You were the one who wanted to stay here. We both knew most of the opportunities in my field were in New York, but you insisted on staying here for your goddamned arts and crafts shop."

"It's not a goddamned arts and crafts shop," Anne said, bristling.

"I don't know what the hell it is," he continued. "It's a front to create the illusion you're a businesswoman, isn't it? You support it with family money."

"You bastard." Anne was steaming.

"You controlling bitch," Jonathan pressed on. "The New York issue is just a smokescreen for your desire to control me and dictate the terms of our relationship."

With this Anne began to cry. I felt badly for them. It is always painful to watch people savage one another. How had things gotten so quickly out of hand?

Softening, Jonathan apologized. "I'm sorry. I got carried away."

As her tears subsided Anne said, with weary frustration, "This is what we do. All the time. It's awful. That's why we're here."

"It's worse at home," Jonathan added apologetically, both of them now looking at me.

"I'm sure it is," I said sympathetically, knowing this always to be the case. Then I added, "Does it ever get physical?"

"No. Oh no, never," Jonathan answered, taken aback. Anne gestured in agreement.

I had not meant to frighten them with the question. In the last decade, psychiatrists have become more sensitized to domestic violence. Nowadays, one inquires about it reflexively. Both of them stared at me, wondering what I would say next. As is standard fare in couples therapy, I proceeded to set a few ground rules. Since they came to me because they could not discuss and resolve things together civilly, the first order of business was that things had to remain civilized in here. Of course, they could make it clear how angry or hurt they were, but it had to be within the bounds of reasonable discourse.

Both of them nodded in agreement. They seemed relieved. I felt more like a referee than a therapist, as I often do working with couples. In calmer tones they proceeded to enumerate a litany of problems, including housework, chores, money issues, and dealing with their respective families. Although I had had to call a halt to their explosion, it was actually more valuable than this sanitized discussion in portraying the state of their relationship.

How forcefully a couple enters the therapist's office, I reflected. It is one thing for an individual to come in and tell you about fighting with their partner, quite another to have them arrive and begin fighting in front of you. The immediacy is wrenching. You feel palpably caught up in their anguish and distress.

I looked at them both a little more closely. Jonathan was sitting deep in his chair, arms crossed, head cocked back a bit, as if to gain added distance. As Anne spoke, Jonathan looked back and forth, intently, from her to me. Anne sat erect in her chair, was articulate, and even lively at times. She had regained her composure and confidence. But, I thought to myself, how quickly they had been eroded.

When Anne and Jonathan had completed a description of their conflicts I asked a number of questions about areas they had not covered. As part of taking an inventory of the relationship I asked about their sexual life.

"It's great," said Anne. "He's the best lover I've ever

had." She cast a glance at Jonathan who was quick to agree on the quality of their sex life.

"No complaints," he said.

In fact they gave the impression it was their sex life that was holding the relationship together. Both of them had previous sexual partners. Anne alluded to having had more sexual experience than Jonathan.

I asked each of them whether or not they thought the relationship would survive. Both expressed a desire to work things out but they had grave doubts about whether or not this was possible.

"We've said things to one another that are so hurtful, I sometimes wonder if we can ever get past this," said Anne. "Then at other times I remember how good things were, the wonderful times we had, and I think we must be able to recoup that."

Curious about the better times, I inquired in our second meeting about the history of their relationship: What brought them together? What was their relationship like early on? Sure enough, they described a very different state of affairs. They met at an art gallery opening. Through family connections Anne knew the gallery owner and frequently attended such events. Jonathan was a friend of the artist. Both were undergraduates at the time they met—she at a liberal arts college, he at a neighboring art school. They were opposites attracting: She was the outgoing daughter of a prominent Californian family. He was the eccentric computer whiz cum art student from a modest background. They shared a sense of humor and a curiosity about their obvious differences.

As students they felt like voyeurs and interlopers into each other's worlds. Anne took Jonathan to expensive restaurants, opening nights, and fund-raisers. Jonathan took

Anne to offbeat cafés, underground jazz clubs, and the studio lofts of his artist friends. All the while a bond grew between them of shared humor, intimacy, and caring. At the time, there were only occasional suggestions of competition and control issues.

Over the objections of Anne's family, they decided to live together after college. Anne had already planned to open an art gallery in an upscale part of town. Setting up the gallery consumed all of Anne's energy and time in their first year of living together. Meanwhile, Jonathan set out on a career in the movies. He was in the right place at the right time. Computers were revolutionizing the technical end of motion picture production. With his art and computer background he quickly rose from obscurity, becoming one of the most sought-after film editors on the East Coast.

Both of them described "waking up" at the end of that first year out of college with their lives and relationship altogether different from what they had been. Gone were the romantic, private weekends together, the unhurried student pace, the intimacy, and the relaxed communication. In their place were the hectic world of business and demanding careers, too little time, and a growing sense of competition and frustration with one another. In their second year of living together, the tension mounted to its current level of antagonism. Jonathan's success continued, but Anne became disillusioned with her work. While her gallery provided a certain focus and cachet, the administrative details were a burden. Life as a gallery owner was not turning out as she expected.

After listening to their history I thought it was Jonathan's success that upset the equilibrium in the relationship. Before that, the two were mutually dependent, each providing the other with something he or she did not have. But now, while Jonathan's success provided him with his own resources and social connections, Anne had become dissatisfied with her work. A tense, competitive atmosphere arose between them. As a couple, they had not renegotiated their relationship. Would the relationship survive? Would the original connection prevail or would it be overwhelmed by the gathering storm? As yet, they had said nothing about their sexual dysfunction.

In our third meeting, the couples therapy went awry. Anne and Jonathan were late and it was clear they had been arguing. The argument spilled over into the room, the issue being Jonathan's reluctance to participate in the therapy. Jonathan had not wanted to come that evening, Anne reported. He was backing out of the therapy, another example, in her mind, of his defaulting on the relationship.

"I never made a commitment to the therapy," Jonathan said impatiently.

He was originally pressured into coming and did not want to continue. As he spoke, it was evident he viewed the therapy, and therefore me, as an agent of Anne's, a means by which she hoped to hold the relationship together on her terms. He wanted no part of therapy. He viewed the simple act of coming to the sessions as submitting to her, and he did not plan to continue.

Reassurances on my part—I did not intend to side with either of them, I was neutral as to whether or not the relationship held together, and I saw my role as a catalyst in helping them resolve their differences—had little effect. Anne insisted she would stay on in therapy whether Jonathan did or not, a threat she seemed to hope would prompt him to stay. But to no avail. Sparks flew in another heated exchange between them. Which one of them was right? Was Jonathan backing out of the therapy? His reluctance had been obvious in our first meeting but we had not discussed it outright. Why was he unwilling to make the effort she was? Or was she pushing for something he never said he would do? Had she manipulated the situation as he alleged?

In the heat of the moment such questions seemed a luxury. I certainly would not get straightforward answers to them now. The tension escalated to the point that Jonathan threatened to get up and leave. In one last attempt to salvage the couples work, I suggested individual meetings with them both. Perhaps there were things they would find easier to discuss one on one. Jonathan was quick to decline. Clearly his mind was made up, I thought. To push any further could be counterproductive, diminishing any chance he might one day return. By the end of the meeting it was agreed Jonathan would not continue. If he was so inclined, he could return at any point in the future.

Anne returned the next week appearing somewhat deflated.

"I'm disappointed Jonathan's not here," she said as she sat down.

Had she failed in her relationship? Was it falling apart? Had I failed to hold the couples therapy together? Or was Jonathan impossible for the moment, too hurt and defensive?

Initially, Anne was full of recrimination for Jonathan: his aloofness, his unwillingness to deal with feelings, and his lack of commitment. For a few meetings she focused on his history and how she thought it related to his behavior in their relationship. She thought of him as a bohemian when they first met. She had no idea how ambitious he was. He grew up with very little. His father was a grocer and his mother had to work to help support the family. Since Anne had known him, he had turned into a workaholic, determined to escape his past, even at the expense of their relationship.

Gradually, Anne began to talk about herself. She was from a wealthy San Francisco family, the second of four children, and the only daughter. Her parents' marriage was, at best, convenient. Her father and mother came from similar backgrounds but otherwise had little in common. She described her father as a "tyrant," a businessman, and the dominating influence in the household.

"He was always in a rage," she said. "Over anything. Even trivial incidents. Once our cat jumped up on the counter and accidentally knocked over a glass of water. First he threw the screaming cat out the back door. Then he flew around the house until he found someone to blame, in this instance one of my brothers, whose glass of water it had been. He dragged my brother downstairs by the collar, ranting and raving the whole way, and made him clean it up. You could hear my mother moaning in the background 'Bob, it's okay. I'll clean it up.' But he would have no part of it. We all lived in terror of him."

Anne's mother took the brunt of her father's verbal abuse. Anne described her mother as a passive, ineffectual, but warm woman who had provided the children with the only nurturing they had. But she had been unable to stand up to the father who was consistently disparaging of her, women in general, and therefore, Anne by association, although never directly. To his daughter, he was patronizing rather than condescending, but she felt it was in the same spirit.

Her mother was an emotional invalid, Anne said, after years of being incessantly demeaned. She recalled always taking her mother's side against her father. He would sometimes back off if confronted vigorously enough by his daughter. Her mother had been a "Sunday painter," this being her one refuge from the father, but in her later years, she gave even that up. With her children grown, she had few outside activities and spent most of her time at home in the company of a few domestics. She accompanied her husband on social occasions but in general lead a constricted, passive life.

As a child, Anne feared her father but also desperately wanted his attention. He had a much easier time relating to men than women. With her brothers, he was hard-driving and demanding but attentive to their efforts in school and sports. He seemed not to know what to do with a daughter, not pushing her too hard, but also not expecting much of her.

Her brothers did not fare well from the father's pressure-cooker attention. Two were failed businessmen, and the third was "lost" to drugs and an endless adolescent rebellion against the father. In retrospect, Anne realized ironically, her father's neglect spared her a similar fate. She was the only one who had been successful academically. Her father sometimes referred to her as his "consolation prize." While she enjoyed being prized by him, she resented the second-rate implication.

As I listened to Anne I wondered, What was she doing in business? I suspected she was still trying to get her father's attention, to prove herself to him. Yet she was disillusioned with her business and unsatisfied. I thought she was deeply conflicted about her relationship to her father. As a daughter she would never be fully valued by him. Yet, had she been a son he would have undermined her like her brothers.

What was her fascination with art? Why was she in a relationship with an artist and in her professional life promoting the work of other artists? How much did it have to do with protecting her mother, the Sunday painter? Art seemed to represent a connection with her mother, which she approached vicariously through Jonathan and her work but was fearful of embracing herself.

Beginning in high school, Anne took "refuge" in a series of sexual relationships.

"Some of them were with guys I was dating, others were completely secretive," she said.

"How do you mean *refuge*?" I asked.

"Things at home were at their worst when I was in high school. My father had business problems and was more difficult than ever. That's around when my mother gave up. You could see what little willpower she had left caving in. I had to get out of the house. I discovered sex as an outlet for my frustrations and a way to be appreciated by men. I've had more sexual partners than I care to remember."

"You feel guilty about it?"

"No. I just wish it hadn't been necessary."

Before Jonathan, Anne had not had a monogamous relationship.

"My relationship with Jonathan, before it deteriorated, was definitely the best I've ever had, sexually and otherwise," she said.

Anne's father objected strenuously to her living with Jonathan, who was too offbeat for his tastes. He did not think an artist was good enough for his daughter. To him, the arts were just something to donate money to for a tax deduction. He liked to be seen at the right openings and to be known in social circles as a patron. But beyond that art meant nothing to him.

As we talked, several insights emerged regarding Anne's relationship to Jonathan. First, she was fearful of the relationship breaking up because "her father would have been right." Second, in the relationship with Jonathan she was to a strong degree rebelling and asserting herself against her father. Third, and most upsetting, was a realization that her relationship to Jonathan bespoke an identification with her father.

"I suppose it was my own form of patronage," she said. "He was more of a starving artist when I first met him. I enjoyed providing for him. When the balance of the relationship shifted I guess I felt at a loss." With tears in her eyes, Anne continued, "You can't imagine how upset that makes me feel, to think I'm like my father. That's the last thing I would want in my life."

I felt tremendous sympathy for Anne who had made it clear how much she disliked this man. Of course, she was sick at the thought of being like him. At the same time, I felt a sense of relief. For some time Anne had been describing painful family events with little accompanying emotion. The emergence of her feelings was a turning point.

In the ensuing weeks she became increasingly depressed, often a necessary stage in psychotherapy. She mentioned with some surprise that the fighting with Jonathan "actually decreased in spite of how awful" she was feeling. I explained this was not unusual: When people get more in touch with their feelings, they have less of a need to act them out.

It was in this depressed phase of the work, at about the three-month mark, that Anne was talking in one meeting about wanting to have a baby.

"I know I want one for all the wrong reasons," she said. "I'm bored. I'm frustrated. I want one to fill my life. I want one to save the relationship. It wouldn't be fair to the child."

"How do you mean *to save the relationship*?" I asked.

"You want to have a baby to hold onto the relationship with Jonathan?"

"No," she said. "I'm not worried about that. I don't worry about Jonathan leaving. I want a baby to give meaning back to our relationship."

Why, I asked, was she not concerned about Jonathan's leaving?

"I'm just not," she said. "I never worry about his having affairs or anything, even with all the time he spends in New York."

I was perplexed. Why was she so sure he would not leave? She seemed so confident, but on what basis? As a therapist one learns to push those small, jarring incongruities. Behind them often lie larger issues.

"Why aren't you concerned?" I asked again. "I thought one of the big problems was his growing independence."

Somewhat sheepishly she answered, "I'm not worried about his having affairs because he . . . ," she faltered and then continued, "he comes too quickly."

I looked at her quizzically.

"He comes too fast. What do you call it? He's a . . . premature ejaculator."

Imagine my surprise that this man, who she once said was her "best lover ever," was a premature ejaculator.

"He is?" I said.

"Yes. So he hasn't got much confidence when it comes to women."

If Jonathan had difficulty with premature ejaculation, why had Anne said he was the best lover she ever had, I asked.

Anne seemed taken aback that I remembered this small detail and said defensively, "I'm not sure I want to get into it."

"Why not?"

"Because that gets into my own sexual performance."

"You also have a problem?"

Anne hesitated, embarrassed, and then said bluntly, "I don't have an orgasm during intercourse."

"That doesn't explain how he's the best lover."

"Well, he's the first person I have had an orgasm with, only still not during intercourse."

"How do you mean?"

"I experience orgasm during oral sex with Jonathan. Lots of other guys had done that for me before but I never reached orgasm with any of them."

I never cease to be amazed, although I have seen it many times before: Here was a sexually liberated individual, with considerable experience, who reported her current sex life as "great," yet she never had an orgasm during intercourse. Sexual liberation is no guarantee of the freedom to enjoy.

In subsequent meetings, Anne and I discussed her sexual history. Before Jonathan, she could not have an orgasm at all in the presence of a partner. The problem was not that Anne was unresponsive sexually, disinterested, or frigid. She masturbated from a young age, always enjoyed it, and easily reached orgasm by this method. She also had no problem being sexually aroused and fully stimulated—fully lubricated—with a sexual partner. Her previous lovers were fully competent sexually and many made, in her words, "heroic efforts" to bring her to orgasm. They would prolong intercourse for extended periods of time, try a variety of positions, and provide manual or oral stimulation to bring her to orgasm, all "to no avail." As Anne said, summarizing the efforts of her previous lovers, "It's been a Sisyphean task."

It was a paradox that Jonathan, in spite of his sexual limitations, was the first to bring Anne to orgasm, albeit by a method other than intercourse.

"I don't think he did anything differently," she said. "It's just that when we had oral sex it worked."

I suspected there was more to the paradox, something about Jonathan's limitation that allowed her to reach orgasm in his presence. But it would be some time before we were able to puzzle this out. Pursuing the subject from a different angle, I asked if her ability to orgasm had changed at all recently.

"Yes, it has," she said. "In the last seven or eight months I don't reach orgasm at all, which upsets Jonathan. It was one thing that made him feel competent in bed. We don't sleep together much any more."

Now I thought I better understood Jonathan's defensive stance in our meetings.

"Is this part of why he left therapy?" I asked.

"Probably," said Anne. "I think he was afraid of it coming out. He's very embarrassed by it. I guess I trust you enough by now; I thought you should know."

Since the 1960s, specific behavioral techniques, pioneered by Masters and Johnson, have been available for the treatment of sexual dysfunction. The question thus arose whether or not I should refer Anne and Jonathan for such treatment, concurrent with Anne's individual psychotherapy.

Such a decision is not necessarily made lightly. All too often, psychiatrists and other therapists divide into camps— analysts, psychotherapists, psychopharmacologists, and behaviorists, to name just a few—with rigid ideological boundaries. To make such a referral would certainly alter my psychological work with Anne, just at a point when it was deepening. The concurrent sex therapy would naturally become a predominant theme. Should I wait and let the individual therapy develop further before introducing this adjunct?

For me there was really no question: Anything that might help should be tried and added without delay. To facilitate Anne and Jonathan's getting practical help with their sexual difficulties would strengthen my relationship with Anne and potentially relieve them both of considerable distress. Indeed, as it turned out, the sex therapy potentiated the psychotherapy: In the process of treating the couple's sexual difficulties, the psychological issues Anne and I had been working on would unravel.

When I broached the subject of sex therapy with Anne, she expressed interest and surprise that specific treatment was available. Jonathan accompanied her to the next appointment, intrigued by this new development. He was much more eager and responsive than in our previous encounters. His posture was strikingly different: He leaned forward and gestured as he asked questions. Even before this turn of events, he said he had been feeling more favorably toward therapy because of the improvement in the couple's relationship in recent months.

In response to their questions I explained how sex therapy would work. They would be instructed in a graduated series of exercises, or techniques, designed to reverse their sexual dysfunctions. The exercises would not be practiced or demonstrated in the therapist's office. Rather, Anne and Jonathan would practice at home and report back on their progress. Using these techniques, premature ejaculation is curable virtually 100 percent of the time. Orgasmic problems respond roughly 80 percent of the time. I told them the combination of a man with premature ejaculation and a woman with orgasmic difficulties is not uncommon in the area of sexual dysfunction. The two are treated sequentially, the man's first, since his competence is required to work on hers.

Like Anne's, Jonathan's sexual dysfunction was long-standing. His ejaculatory urgency dated to his earliest sexual experiences, which were hurried affairs in the back seats of cars. The first time he had intercourse with a girlfriend was in a parked car in front of her parents' house. They had not planned on going that far sexually and both were terrified the girl's father would come out at any minute. Circumstances were not much better for Jonathan's next few sexual encounters, and by then the pattern was set. Jonathan's history is not uncommon among men with poor ejaculatory control, evidence of the early malleability of the human sexual response, how quickly patterns are established, and once established, how tenacious they become.

With my encouragement, Anne and Jonathan began sex therapy with a therapist I referred them to. Anne kept me informed of the progress of the sex therapy and the other therapist and I spoke periodically to coordinate our efforts. When all goes well, the two therapeutic modalities become reciprocal and synergistic influences.

At the heart of Jonathan's treatment were "start-stop" techniques with manual or oral stimulation to heighten his arousal just short of orgasm. At the first premonition of orgasm, the man signals the woman to stop stimulation. Once preorgasmic urgency has waned, stimulation resumes. This pattern of stimulation is practiced repeatedly. Gradually, the man becomes more aware of the sensations leading up to ejaculation and establishes mastery over delaying it.

As the sex therapy proceeds, psychological issues related

to the sexual dysfunction inevitably emerge. The psychological issues must be dealt with if they would otherwise be an impediment to resolution of the sexual problems. Going into sex therapy, Anne expressed some ambivalence. After all, the sexual dysfunction first came up in the context of her not worrying Jonathan would stray because of his inadequacies. To treat their sexual limitations was to further disrupt the equilibrium in the relationship, however unhealthy the equilibrium may have been.

In the early weeks of the couple's sex therapy, I could see the strain it placed on Anne. In our sessions, she was uncharacteristically short-tempered and irritable. It was not easy for her to be supportive and encouraging of Jonathan's emancipation from his problem. Still, I admired her courage. Although ambivalent, she was determined to facilitate his progress.

By the third week, Jonathan was able to maintain an erection for several minutes with manual stimulation. Anne was clearly anxious reporting this.

"He's rising to the occasion," she quipped. She realized for the first time that Jonathan was going to succeed. Before this she had not fully believed in the efficacy of the sex therapy.

Jonathan's progress caused Anne to remember a forgotten pattern with her former boyfriends. She recalled she used to get angry at her previous lovers when they had an orgasm.

"I made it clear I resented their orgasms," she said. She could also be quite vocal about the fact that she did not reach orgasm. "I tried to make it their problem, their failure." Often she would get into a foul mood after sex. One boyfriend eventually said that although sex with her was great, it was not worth it because she was so nasty afterward. Anne related all this with considerable regret. I could sense her shifting psychologically, moving toward a realignment of her feelings and attitudes about sex. Here the behavioral changes, resulting from the sex therapy, were dislodging psychic issues.

A few weeks later Jonathan reached yet another milestone: He was able to maintain an erection intravaginally for several minutes. In Anne's psychotherapy I could see further psychic stress and dividends. For the first time, Anne said definitively that she had not really been unhappy with the previous status quo in their sexual relationship. Unlike with previous lovers, she never complained to Jonathan. Rather, she thought their sexual relationship was a big improvement over anything she had before.

"It's strange I so readily accepted his disability," she said. "Now that it's going away, I realize I may have even liked it."

"Why might you have liked it?" I asked.

"That's what I've been trying to figure out. I don't know. He could never have satisfied me . . . being unable to last any length of time. Yet he satisfied me more than anybody. It's confusing."

"What effect did his disability have on how you felt sexually?"

Anne thought for a moment and then shook her head.

"What are you thinking?" I asked.

"I thought of something when you asked the question but it's so objectionable I didn't want to say it. I've been trying to find something else to say, but I can't."

"What did you think?"

"That it was easier for me to be tender and caring with Jonathan because he was impaired. This sounds awful but I think his being compromised made me feel I had the upper hand." Anne sat dazed for a few moments, shocked by what she had said. Then she collected herself and went on, "You know, I think that's why I was able to reach orgasm with him during oral sex. I felt less competitive. I didn't resent his orgasm so much. His lack of control made his orgasm ... devalued."

Anne again voiced discomfort with what she was discovering. This is a difficult aspect of psychotherapy, and I expressed support for her efforts to get to the bottom of things.

"I think, perhaps, I stopped experiencing orgasm with Jonathan during oral sex because, maybe, in general ... he'd become more of a threat."

Now it was clear how the sexual issues were a metaphor for the larger issues troubling the relationship. Anne and I explored the now apparent parallels: Early on in the relationship Anne felt an edge over Jonathan because of her financial resources and social connections. Similarly, in the sexual domain, she felt an edge because of his sexual dysfunction. Naturally inclined to be competitive with men because of her relationship with her brothers and father, her competitiveness was dampened at the interpersonal level by Jonathan's financial limitations and at the sexual level by his impairment. Indeed, Jonathan's wounded status elicited from her a tenderness and caring, even the freedom to have an orgasm in his presence, which she had not known before.

Jonathan's financial and social success tipped the scales in their relationship, making him "a threat." Their relationship became quarrelsome and competitive. Sexually, Anne withdrew and was no longer able to have an orgasm with him. The sexual movements exquisitely reflected the larger tensions between them.

Might Anne have still chosen the right man for the

wrong reasons? Was this a hurdle she had to work through, learning to relate to a less dependent Jonathan? Was the task to work out more of a partnership, a more reciprocal relationship with a man than she had known in her family of origin?

Working out such a relationship was precisely what she was doing in sex therapy. Here she was called on to facilitate Jonathan's growth and development. Of course, this felt like a great risk. But if the relationship survived, it also held tremendous potential. If Anne and Jonathan could work things out on a sexual level, the gains might generalize.

Armed with these insights, Anne made it through the last lap of Jonathan's sex therapy more smoothly. In fact, she gave of herself generously. After eight weeks of consistent work on their part, Anne reported they had "licked his premature ejaculation, no pun intended." Jonathan reached his goal of being able to delay ejaculation during intercourse for twenty minutes.

"Of course I'm happy for him," she said apprehensively. "But the problem is it shifts the focus to me."

One would have hoped the insights gained while working on Jonathan's sexual dysfunction would make the treatment of Anne's that much easier, but this proved not to be the case. Neither of us anticipated her even greater ambivalence would arise trying to resolve her own sexual dysfunction.

In Jonathan and Anne's sexual relationship, his premature ejaculation had masked her orgasmic difficulties. A woman cannot be expected to reach orgasm if her partner is unable to sustain intercourse for a reasonable length of time. To her credit, Anne had not hidden her sexual dysfunction from Jonathan, but it was never an issue between them because of his limitations. Now that Jonathan's competence was established, Anne's problems moved to center stage.

The exercises for orgasmic dysfunction are designed to prolong and enhance the woman's sexual pleasure. The goal is to heighten her arousal and lower her orgasmic threshold. The behavioral panoply of intercourse is broken down into a series of small steps: extragenital foreplay, genital foreplay, penile insertion, containment of the penis, slow pelvic thrusting, and vigorous pelvic thrusting. Each step is focused on in turn, taking time for the woman to develop a rich awareness of the sensations. When, after weeks, the couple arrive at pelvic thrusting, it is at a slow, nondemanding pace. Orgasm is explicitly not the goal. Instead, the focus remains on the woman's losing herself in the sensual experience. Control of all activity, positions, and timing rests with the woman who is given "permission to be selfish." Focusing the woman's attention on her sensory experience distracts her from her usual focus, which is to step outside herself and anxiously watch, or "spectator," her sexual performance, leading to its further deterioration. Paradoxically, if the woman's focus is on whether or not she will have an orgasm it is much less likely to happen. If she can be persuaded to lose herself in the sexual sensations, the orgasm may just follow.

Anne's initial reaction was that there was little in her exercises that she had not tried before with one or another partner. She was subtly disparaging of her sex therapy, whereas she had not been with Jonathan's. Nevertheless, Anne proceeded for the first weeks, saying she hoped the exercises would work for her as they had for him. But by the third week, she was showing increasing evidence of impatience and reluctance. She began to compare herself unfavorably with Jonathan and complained of her relative lack of progress in contrast to what had been his steady, incremental gains.

The sex therapist explained to Anne, and I reinforced, that it was a mistake to compare her sexual dysfunction and its treatment with Jonathan's; they were of a quite different nature. Rather, she should only compare herself with herself; that is, to her previous level of function and her progress toward her goal. In their meetings, the sex therapist looked for problems with the couple's technique, their communication, or subtle sabotaging messages they might be sending one another. But the sex therapist could find nothing to account for Anne's growing discouragement.

In the third and fourth weeks of her treatment, Anne's discontent with the sex therapy escalated. In our meetings she refused to discuss the psychological aspects of the developing impasse so long as the exercises were ongoing. She seemed really to be backing out of her sex therapy against all advice. I speculated aloud in our meetings about why she was not giving herself the benefit of the same treatment Jonathan received, instead of selling herself short. Nevertheless, Anne insisted she wanted the sex therapy to stop.

As is usually the case when someone is backing out of a part of a therapeutic program, a flurry of activity ensued. The sex therapist called to see if I understood what Anne was doing, which I did not.

Jonathan requested to come with Anne to one of her individual psychotherapy meetings. He felt badly she was abandoning her treatment and guilty that his, by contrast, had been successful. However, he had a defensive tone and was applying too much pressure.

"Why," Jonathan asked Anne, "aren't you letting me reciprocate?"

"I'm sorry," said Anne, "but that's not the issue. I can't. It's just not working for me."

I pointed out to Jonathan that while his intentions might be good, he was suggesting Anne continue her treatment to meet his needs: to alleviate his guilt and allow him to reciprocate. His pressure was unlikely to help the situation. Jonathan seemed to understand and was somewhat appeased. The remainder of the meeting went more smoothly but provided no new answers.

So, one month after Anne's sex therapy began, it abruptly ended at her insistence. Although her agitation served as a warning, this still came as a surprise. What was she afraid of, I wondered? What issue loomed so large as to necessitate her stopping the sex therapy?

In our next session, Anne defended her actions, asserting, "I don't think my problems are mechanical. I've been on top, I've used my hand, I've had guys who could last thirty minutes. . . . It's all in my head."

"Well, if it's in your head," I asked, "what do you think is the problem?"

Thus began a series of discussions about the psychological dimensions of Anne's sexual dysfunction. Behavioral treatment had not worked for her and once again the individual psychotherapy stood on its own. The discussions, which took place over months, were intermixed with other acute events and issues and only gradually built to some conclusion.

"I'm afraid of the vulnerability," was her response the first time we discussed it. "I'm afraid of letting go like that. Of losing myself."

"In an orgasm?"

"Yes."

This is not an uncommon theme. Many women, and some men as well, are afraid of losing their minds, being overwhelmed, or being trapped in a relationship if they have an orgasm with a partner. But in exploring this further with Anne, none of these themes developed. She was still heavily defended, I thought. Were none of these themes present? Or were they repressed? She had at one time been able to reach orgasm with Jonathan during oral sex, I pointed out to her.

"But that's different," she replied.

"How so?"

"I don't know. I just assume it is, obviously not based on experience. There's something there. I don't know what it is."

For the time being it remained a mystery.

The next time we discussed it, the conversation took a different turn.

"I think I'm not ready yet," Anne said.

"What do you mean?"

"To reach orgasm during intercourse. I think I'm saving it. Jonathan's not the right one."

"Saving it?"

"Yes. For the right guy. The guy I would marry and spend the rest of my life with."

"Like some women save their virginity?"

Anne laughed. "Well, yes. I guess you could put it that way." After thinking about it briefly, she added with more enthusiasm, "Yes, I'm saving it for Mr. Right. And I'm just not sure at this point Jonathan is the one."

Here was another of the many paradoxes and twists in Anne's case. By any traditional standards she was a woman who had gone all the way. Yet she was holding back, saving something for a special person. What kind of postliberation, postmodern irony was this? Was it true or was it a rationalization?

"Why would you hold back?" I asked. "You're not under any social pressure, like women used to be to preserve their virginity. You let yourself go this far. Your boyfriends, like Jonathan, know your sexual history. Why would you be holding back?"

Anne did not have an answer.

My mind then wandered to all the arcane rituals by which virginity was demonstrated on a wedding night. The timely wandering of the therapist's mind is an interesting phenomenon in psychotherapy. Ideally, you stumble into fertile ground and ask an odd question that sets things in motion. My musing over nuptial rites lead me to wondering: If one elevated orgasm to a position formerly held by virginity, how would the man know?

"How," I asked as we ended the session, "will he know he's the first?"

"I don't know," Anne said. "I've never thought of it."

The next week Anne said, "It's not just a matter of saving my orgasm for someone," she said. "It's a question of surrender."

"Surrender?"

"Yes. That's what I was thinking this week. That's what I wanted to tell you."

Could she explain further, I asked.

After thinking for a few minutes, Anne answered, "You see, if it's surrender, it's a. . . ." She struggled and then articulated, "It's a power issue."

"A power issue."

"Yes. Let me put it this way. I thought a lot about the question you asked at the end of last week. About how the guy would know? I'd never thought of it before, but when I did, I quickly realized: Of course, he'd know, because I'd tell him."

"You'd tell him."

"Sure, because that's the whole point. I'd have saved it for him." Anne was speaking a little excitedly now with an air of anticipation. "I think that's it," she said.

I looked at her curiously.

"I'd have saved it for him because . . . it's a gift."

"A gift?"

"Yes, that's my bottom line. It's a gift!"

Anne surprised even herself. The idea had not occurred to her consciously before. Over the course of several meetings, she went on to elaborate. She thought Jonathan and all of her previous lovers had wanted to deliver her to orgasm. To do so would have been a "trophy."

I asked how much she thought the men entered the relationships wanting this trophy versus how much they took up the cause in response to her protests over not having an orgasm. She said that was a good question. It was difficult to sort out, and the men had differed in this regard. But in the end, all the sexual relationships had come to the same point.

Anne was not afraid she would be abandoned if the man succeeded. Rather, her anger and resentment at men made her invested in it not happening. She reiterated her bitterness over the male-female split in her family and her feeling that in society at large she "met more of the same" sexism and discrimination.

"To put it bluntly," she said, "Jonathan wants desperately to give me an orgasm during intercourse, and I'm not going to let him have that."

One of the most challenging aspects of doing long-term psychotherapy is that just when you reach "the answer," the struggle begins. I could already hear the transference implications of what Anne said, but for the moment, she wanted to hear my response.

I said it was unfortunate Anne had been cornered into such a position sexually. To be operating on the equation that her orgasm was a gift to the man was a no-win situation. To have an orgasm was to give him more than she gave herself. To not reach orgasm was to continue to deprive herself. It was a self-defeating formula.

I went on to say I could imagine some of her sexual partners came into the relationship viewing her orgasm as a trophy. But her response to that might have been to become disinterested in them. Instead, she agreed she was invested in the scenario.

Her current state of affairs was indeed proof that the power was ultimately hers. It was she who decided not to reach orgasm during intercourse, and it would be she who gave herself permission to, were the situation to change. Likewise, to allow herself to have an orgasm would be a far greater gift to herself than to the man. By not experiencing orgasm, she was losing out far more than he.

I was concerned that Anne had internalized devalued images of womanhood and was punishing herself, perpetuating in her self-deprivation the very disparities she tried to fight against. The prejudices she perceived in her family and in society were real, but how could the response be to punish her lover and, even more so, herself in bed?

I added that whether she ultimately stayed with Jonathan or not mattered little to this issue in the long run. The issue had more to do with her relationship to herself than it did to her relationship to him. If she could allow herself the shared pleasure of orgasm, it could only enhance the possibility the relationship would survive. If the relationship did not, she would take the accomplishment with her into future relationships. It would not be a trophy she would leave behind with him.

Anne listened to and debated the points carefully. At times the debate got heated, which was a wonderful thing. These are not arid ideas but emotional issues. Ultimately, it is at an emotional level that people get stuck and it takes emotion to move them.

For the moment Anne was not moved.

"This is all well and good," she said somewhat flippantly in one session. "I can see some of your points, but it's not going to happen. Not yet anyway."

"Well, of course it's not," I said, overstating the case. "If it were this easy it would have changed long ago. And in the end it has to be your decision."

I overstated the case because this was such a crucial juncture. We had reached the transference, often one of the most important parts of a long-term psychotherapy. The concept of transference was one of Freud's greatest contributions to the field. In transference, the patient transfers their core issues onto the relationship with the therapist. Anne was digging in her heels, saying she was not about to reach orgasm, although she held out the possibility of change. She was setting up her having an orgasm with Jonathan as an issue in the therapy. Would I struggle with her over whether or not she changed? Or would I decline the gambit?

Here I had a choice. The Freudian position would be to interpret the transference for her, to point out that she was creating a struggle over whether or not she changed, putting me in a role not unlike her lovers'. The alternative, which I chose, was a more experiential approach advocated by American psychiatrist Harry Stack Sullivan. If Anne's lovers struggled with her over her orgasm, why would I do the same? The idea here is that when therapy and an unhealthy pattern in a patient's life intersect, it is crucial to do things differently. If Anne got the impression I was invested in her having an orgasm for my esteem as a therapist, we would be repeating the deadlock with the lover in the bedroom. I was concerned any interpretive or confrontational approach would get us into such an impasse. So my simple, but I hoped powerful, response was to throw the ball back into her court. I wanted to give the clear impression I cared, but not to a counterproductive degree; of course, I would love for her to feel free to have an orgasm, but for her sake, not mine. Ultimately, she could only change for herself, not for me.

We went over these issues again and again for many months. It is during these months of therapy that I think of change as percolating in the patient's consciousness. People do not change overnight as the result of insights, except in the movies. There are occasions when a person comes in with something fairly circumscribed and the timing is just right to precipitate change quickly. But those occasions are rare. Most often, in real life, it takes time. One has to repeatedly go over the same ground. The therapist is always testing to see if there are more layers, further depths. At the same time, the patient is examining the therapist's responses over and over again to look for any inconsistencies, testing the sincerity of what the therapist says and feels, before incorporating it and making fundamental life changes.

During this time, Anne made changes in a number of other areas. Most important was the decision to sell her gallery and go to art school, a decision she contemplated for many months. She wanted, as she said, "to do her own work instead of promoting the work of others." She felt vulnerable and scared about "putting herself on the line." She would have less control over her life and identity as a fledgling artist, but she was ready to try. Anne's appearance also changed. Although always quite lively, she had had a somewhat plastic, too fashionable look. As her life-style changed she became more individual in appearance as well as in personality.

Some six months after our last lengthy discussion of the sexual issues, Anne casually reported in one meeting that for about a month she had been reaching orgasm during intercourse with Jonathan roughly 50 percent of the time. A month later she followed up, saying she was experiencing orgasm, often multiple orgasm, during intercourse most of the time.

This kind of change is always remarkable, but one sees it over and over again in psychotherapy. You lay all the groundwork in an area, and then you wait. When the transference hits, you refuse to get caught up in an old, unhealthy pattern. Without rejecting the patient, while hanging in there and making it clear you care, you insist on doing things differently. The relationship has to be intense enough, emotional enough, and powerful enough for you to have an effect. Once you have stated your case, you try to stay out of the patient's way. You leave it to the patient to change in his or her own time. If all goes well, you hear the positive results. Hopefully, the patient has learned a new way of relating, which can be generalized.

Anne continued in therapy for another two years. The gains she and Jonathan made sexually were sustained over time. Although it was not certain at the time Anne left therapy, it appeared she and Jonathan would make a lifelong commitment to each other.

THE ACROBAT'S STOCKING

D avid was out of breath when he arrived at my office. He had run across Harvard Square, he said, fearful of being late for the appointment. Only the day before, he had contacted me for the first time and had expressed some urgency about meeting.

David was an interesting-looking character dressed all in black: sneakers, baggy pants, open shirt, and leather jacket. He was olive-complected with a trim moustache and thick crop of straight hair rising off his forehead. He had an expectant, energetic air.

"I've come to see you about a sexual problem," David said as soon as we sat down. "I can't manage intercourse with a condom. Every time I try to use one, I lose my erection. The reason I needed to see you quickly was because I'm in a new relationship with a woman named Laura. On a few occasions things have progressed sexually almost to the point of intercourse. She's not on the pill and I'll be expected to use a condom. I'm going over to her apartment for dinner after work. I'm pretty sure it's an invitation for more. I think tonight will be the night. . . ."

"I see," I nodded. Then, wanting to dispel any myths, I said, "That would be a lot to solve in one session, don't you think?"

"I suppose so," David laughed. "I'd sure like to, but I guess I don't necessarily expect to."

"Just so that's understood from the start."

"All right," David agreed.

"So you and Laura may sleep together tonight."

"I think she's expecting it."

"And the condom problem will come up."

"Right."

"You've already discussed contraception I take it? That's how you know she's not on the Pill?"

"Yes. She hasn't been in a relationship for a while, so she went off the Pill. She won't go back on it until she's in a steady relationship. A lot of women feel like that, not wanting to stay on the Pill indefinitely because of the risks."

"True."

"Besides, even apart from birth control, nowadays it's expected the man will use a condom for both people's protection. In recent years it's become a lot harder to work around my problem."

"What exactly happens when you try to use a condom?"

Small beads of perspiration had collected on David's forehead. Discussing his problem was anxiety-provoking. He drew the moisture up into his open hand, streaking it through his hair.

"I can't go through with intercourse," he replied. "Sometimes I fumble, losing the erection as I try to put the condom on. At other times I'm able to get it on and enter the woman, but I lose my erection fairly quickly and can't finish what I've begun."

"Do you have trouble maintaining an erection under any other circumstances?"

"No, never."

"Not even occasionally, if you're fatigued or anxious?"

"Sometimes I'm not in the mood to have sex, but I can almost always be seduced into it."

"Have you ever had any other sexual difficulties like coming faster than you want to?"

"No. I've always had good control."

"So you only have trouble wearing a condom? Otherwise everything is okay?"

"Right."

David's problem was intriguing. His difficulty was not a sexual dysfunction in the classic sense of the word, that is, impotence or premature ejaculation. His was something more idiosyncratic and situational.

I first thought of friction as the possible cause. Some men complain they do not get enough friction during intercourse when wearing a condom, depending on the type and brand. Had he tried different ones, I asked.

"I've tried everything. Regular, lubricated, ribbed. It makes no difference. I've even tried pigskin condoms without luck."

In contrast to latex condoms, pigskin ones are made of a natural material and are, therefore, more comfortable and closer to the experience of natural intercourse.

"I don't think the problem is friction," David asserted. "Without a condom on I can last a long time even after a woman is very relaxed and not holding me strongly."

"That may be so but wearing a condom is different," I said.

"I've also slept with women who had really good control over their vaginal muscles and were able to hold me very tightly with a condom on. It didn't make any difference. I've just got this thing about condoms. Some sort of mental block, I guess."

"Do you have any idea what it is?"

"No. That's why I'm here."

I thought a few minutes about David's situation, then asked, "How much of the problem is awkwardness physically putting a condom on?"

"I'm only awkward some of the time, and then it's because I'm anxious. Believe me, I know how to use them. I just can't make them work."

"Have you practiced at home putting them on and taking them off?"

David laughed. "Many times!"

"Do you integrate putting the condom on into your foreplay with a woman? You know, instead of just furtively turning aside to don it?"

"Sure. I've even had the woman, when the time came, put the condom on me. Again it made no difference."

"And you've tried using a condom many times?"

"Literally hundreds of times," David lamented. "Not that I've had that many relationships but I've tried repeatedly in most relationships. It's been so frustrating . . . I can't tell you."

David's frustration with his predicament was evident. However, he was beginning to relax in the session.

"What's your attitude toward being expected to use a condom?" I asked.

"What do you mean?"

"Some men take a chauvinistic position that contraception should be the woman's responsibility. Others are naturalists; they don't want to be encumbered by a rubber."

"No," David said and shook his head. "I don't feel negatively toward condoms. I'd love to be able to use them!"

The problem did not seem to be mechanical or attitudinal vis-à-vis condoms, although I still thought inadequate friction was a possibility. At this point, I asked David to tell me more about his sexual history.

David began by describing his first sexual experience, which he said was "traumatic."

"I grew up in Chicago. Like many people growing up in the Midwest, my summers were spent on a lake. The summer after my sophomore year in high school, I was dating a girl. We hadn't had many dates, just a few, when one night we went down to the beach quite late with another couple. In my back pocket I had a rubber which I'd taken out of my brother's bureau drawer, just in case. But I didn't know what the hell I was doing. At that point I'd never experimented with rubbers, didn't know how to use one, and wasn't really ready to have intercourse.

"Anyway, the four of us had gone down to the lake. It was quite romantic and inspiring. The moonlight reflecting off the water, the tall pines, and white sand were enticing. We separated from the other couple, who went farther down the beach, I thought probably to make love. My girlfriend and I started making out. One thing led to another and before long we were only half-dressed. I was very aroused but not totally into it.

"It was a misty evening, which heightened the romanticism but made the sand sticky. I remember every time we rolled over all this sand would stick to my ass and I didn't like it." David laughed self-consciously. "That didn't suit me. The conditions just weren't right."

This vivid, tactile image was evidence of some obsessionalism. Here David was describing one of his earliest sexual experiences, which took place in an inspiring setting and which would have been intensely arousing. Why was he worrying about the sand sticking to his backside? What conflicts did this obsessional concern mask? Did he not like the woman? Was it her in particular or a fear of women's bodies in general? Was it inexperience and performance anxiety? Did he feel competitive with the other man who had gone farther down the beach?

As if he heard my last thought, David commented on the presence of his friends. "I was aware of Mark and Julie, even though they had gone some distance from us. I was afraid of being halfway through making love only to have them saunter up and ask if we were ready to go. I wasn't really prepared for intercourse but I miscalculated and everything went wrong."

"How do you mean *miscalculated*?"

"I wasn't experienced sexually and I missed the boat on how excited Karen had gotten. We were rolling around passionately on the beach, when suddenly she slipped off her underpants and said, 'Fuck me,' and I lost it."

"You lost it?"

"My erection."

"Yes, of course."

"I guess she thought I was experienced or something, but I didn't know what to do. I fumbled around with the condom, worrying how I would put myself inside her . . . was she going to do that for me? I wasn't prepared to just mount her. It was awful and I went limp."

Poor fellow, I thought. How many times have I heard similar stories from men, the supposedly invulnerable sex? Why do they never show this scene in the movies?

"What happened?" I asked.

"I tried to put the condom on but it was useless. My erection was gone. I was quivering all over the place. It was like trying to put a condom on Jell-O."

I noted again David's colorful, vivid imagery. His initial

anxiety discussing this subject had evaporated. He did not seem the inhibited type at all.

"Karen was pretty good about it," he continued, "although it must have been frustrating for her. I made some lame excuse about feeling self-conscious and not liking the setting. But I was mortified."

The story of David's first sexual encounter raised another possible explanation for his problem: Perhaps condoms were associated with this early trauma and, therefore, always provoked considerable anxiety. David's reaction to this idea was skeptical.

"I suppose if that were the case it would be unconscious on my part, so how can I say for certain it's not true? But I doubt it," he responded. "Since then I've become experienced and confident sexually. I can't imagine this is the legacy of that early experience when I've had no other problems."

David's next sexual experience began the following year in high school and lasted until his graduation, a year and a half later. David began seeing a classmate who was Catholic, whereas he was Jewish. Because of her religion, the woman wanted to keep her virginity. The relationship quickly became sexual and the two began bringing each other to orgasm via oral sex. After high school, they went their separate ways to different colleges and began dating other people. However, for years they got together when home on weekends or vacations to satisfy each other sexually.

"As a result of that relationship," said David jokingly, "I'm an oral sex aficionado. I need to have mutual oral sex with a woman before I have intercourse with her."

"Do you reach orgasm during the oral sex?"

"No, no. It's a preliminary, but kind of a prerequisite.

To me, that's the most intimate you can get with a woman and I like to get past that point before having intercourse."

I thought this a somewhat idiosyncratic notion, another of David's eccentricities.

David said he came into his own sexually during college. He began having intercourse and had a number of sexual partners. He described himself as quite liberal and uninhibited sexually. He also made an effort to "create the right atmosphere" for sex. When I asked what that meant, he said, "I have incense and candles in my room. I like to have a nice wine, sometimes a little food. I had a bit of a reputation in college for being a connoisseur of sex."

"I see."

"Which is why the nagging problem with condoms has been all the more daunting."

Turning from his sexual history to other areas I asked David if he had any medical problems.

"I'm in excellent health," he answered. "I don't get enough exercise but I eat well and stay trim."

"You've had the problem with the condoms for how long?"

"Roughly ten years."

"Has there been any change over the years?"

"None at all. Why do you ask?"

I explained that episodic sexual difficulties can be early, subtle symptoms of medical conditions like diabetes. However, the pattern of David's problem argued against a medical, or physical, cause. A physical problem would either be present more consistently or wax and wane in a more variable pattern, instead of being tied to a specific set of circumstances. Most important, one would expect a progressive deterioration in sexual and other physiological functions over time, which obviously had not happened.

David was not on any medication. His sexual problem was not associated with excessive alcohol intake or other drug use. Chemicals of one sort or another, prescription or otherwise, are a common cause of sexual dysfunction. But not in David's case.

I next asked David about his family and religious background. He grew up in an urban, Jewish enclave in Chicago with a strong ethnic and cultural identity. He described the neighborhood as a mix of blue-collar and lower-middle-class families. His father was the manager of a chain of discount record stores in the Chicago area.

As a child, David would often cross the city after school, going to whichever store his father was working at that day. He went to be with his father, listen to music, and mingle with the patrons and staff.

"I grew interested in becoming an architect," said David of his career, "in those daily treks as a kid, crisscrossing Chicago, home of Frank Lloyd Wright and city of innovation in American architecture."

His being an architect, I thought, fit with his strong visual sense, his palpable imagery.

David said he and his family were a little unusual compared with the rest of their neighborhood. By the time he was ten years old, his parents could have moved to the more affluent suburbs as many of their friends did. However, they chose to stay in their more tightly knit, urban community. David and his siblings, a brother and two sisters, were also unusual because they went off to college and graduate school on the East Coast. Most of his friends stayed closer to home, did not go to college, and went into the family business or started one of their own.

"What was the attitude in your home toward sexuality?" I asked.

"Pretty relaxed. Not that my parents talked much about sex. They did give us books and were willing to discuss it a little."

"How do they feel about premarital sex?"

"They know I'm sexually active and, as far as I know, are quite comfortable with it."

"Did religion have much of an influence on how sexuality was treated?"

"No. My parents were not overly religious. They were more into Jewish culture and tradition. They were pretty liberal. Still are."

I asked a number of other questions that are barometers of the prevailing sexual tone in a family—how nudity was handled in the home, the attitude toward masturbation, and so on—and found nothing out of the ordinary.

On several of these issues I pressed repeatedly, hoping to find some clue of a psychological dimension to David's problem. But none emerged.

I asked David about his own self-image: his masculinity, whether or not he thought he was attractive to women, and how he felt about taking initiative in sexual relationships. He reported no conflicts in these areas.

Still another possibility was conscious or unconscious homosexual wishes. However, David had no homosexual experience and was not sexually attracted to men. I inquired specifically about his dream and fantasy life, even more sensitive measures of sexual desire, but these too were exclusively heterosexual.

Finally, I asked if David had any other early sexual experiences, traumatic or humiliating events, which might have influenced his sexual development. David could not think of anything.

We had covered the range of issues relating to sexuality: sexual history, sexual attitudes and interests, family dynamics, religious background, medical conditions, and drugs. So far we turned up only two slim possibilities—inadequate friction when wearing condoms or an anxiety-provoking association between condoms and the debacle of his first sexual encounter. Two eccentricities, or quirks, also emerged: a tendency to be fussy about the atmosphere he was in and a prerequisite of mutual oral sex with a woman before intercourse. In spite of my early disclaimer, the approaching deadline with Laura hung ever present in the air. With less than half our time remaining, I asked David about Laura and the history of their relationship.

The two met in an evening class they were both attending. They struck up a friendship and began dating once the class was over. They had many interests in common so it had been easy to find things they enjoyed doing together. Thus far the relationship had developed in a natural, relaxed manner.

Just the week earlier they had gone further than ever before sexually.

"I think Laura wanted to make love," said David, "but I've been holding back since I found out she wasn't on any birth control. We're at the point where I'll have to explain to her that I can't use a condom. I hate having to do that. It's embarrassing every time."

"Yet you always try?"

"Yes. I think: Maybe this time it will work. On occasion I've thought I would succeed . . . but have always failed."

"Laura doesn't have a diaphragm?"

"No. I inquired discreetly. Besides, it occasionally happens with a diaphragm."

"You lose your erection?"

"Yes, but not always. It's rare actually, nothing like the problem with a rubber."

This small detail seemed crucial to me. If true, even though rare, it would free the phenomenon from the specific circumstances of a condom. It could be decisive, ruling out for example, the two earlier hypotheses of inadequate friction or an association with David's misfortune the first time he used a condom.

"What exactly happens if the woman uses a diaphragm?" I asked. "Why does it happen sometimes and not others?"

"I'm trying to remember," said David. "I think it has to do with how discreet the woman is about putting the diaphragm in."

"How so?"

"The few times I can recall having a problem the woman hadn't put her diaphragm in before we started to make love. We were pretty close to consummating intercourse when it came up and we had to stop briefly."

"Stopping was the problem?"

"Yes, like the woman has to leave for a minute to put the diaphragm in. . . . Oh, I remember a girlfriend once inserting her diaphragm beside me in bed and that finished me, just like putting a condom on does. But this has happened so few times I can hardly remember."

"I think it may be important," I said, wanting David to make an effort to recall more in this area. "Why don't you have a problem if the woman puts her diaphragm in before you become sexual?"

"Because then I'm not aware of it. It's not an issue."

I was still confused but thought somewhere in this tangle lay the key to David's dilemma.

"You never have a problem if the woman is on the Pill, right?" I asked, beginning to establish a hierarchy of circumstances.

"Never," said David.

"If she inserts a diaphragm before you become sexual, then it's like her being on the Pill: You're not aware of it and there's no problem."

"I hadn't thought of it in those terms before . . . but yes, that's right."

"Whereas if you put a condom on or the woman puts a diaphragm in too late, the problem is you're somehow interrupted too close to intercourse."

"That's it," David nodded.

"What does it mean to you to be interrupted?"

"I don't know. . . . It breaks my stride. I lose my rhythm. I can't get it back."

"Can you say anything more about being interrupted?" I pressed.

David shook his head searching for an answer. Then he broke into a smile.

"What are you thinking?"

"What's coming to mind is an image, a ridiculous image."

"Oh?"

"It's like I'm an acrobat, you know: I jump from a high wire. Climbing up the rope ladder to that little platform and inching my way across the wire is like foreplay. Jumping off is getting really excited. Once I take the leap, I can't be interrupted. There's this incredible rhythm and flow and I can't be distracted.

"As an acrobat I have my routine down perfectly. It's very elaborate, very rhythmical going through my tumbles and twists. Then I'm asked to introduce another element that ruins it: Halfway through the fall I'm supposed to slip a small stocking on my foot. Mechanically it's very simple, nothing by comparison with the choreography of the rest of what I do. But it completely throws me off; it ruins my performance. Every time. I can't manage it."

I was quite taken with David's lively metaphor for his dilemma. What was it about donning a condom, the acrobat's stocking, that destroyed his rhythm and vitality? What intruded on his consciousness to debilitate him? What was it, in that moment, that caused him to lose his nerve, and with it his erection?

"I don't quite understand," I said to David, "all your emphasis on this perfect rhythm and timing that can't be interrupted."

"That's just the way I am," he said a touch defensively.

"Is it like wanting to set the atmosphere and have mutual oral sex before intercourse?"

"Yes. It's all part of how I like to make love."

"It seems a little . . . how can I say it . . . rigid."

"No. I don't think that's the right word," David argued. "I'm still very fluid. I'm not inhibited sexually."

"Well then it's . . . precious."

"Precious?"

"Overprotected. Overwrought. Why can't you take the time to slip on a condom?"

David blanched. "You think I'm precious about sex?"

"Something like that. Why do you have to have it just so? You've mentioned incense, candles, and wine. Your concentration can't be broken for a minute. A prerequisite is mutual oral sex. Why do you have to lavish so much on before intercourse?"

David agitated in his chair. "I don't know. I guess I think one should."

"Should?" I pressed the point.

"I want the woman to know I care."

"Why would she question that?"

"You're asking a lot . . . you know . . . to sleep with her. I don't want my motives to be unclear. I don't want to just jump into intercourse."

"Why not?" I continued provocatively. Why was he bringing up motives? Something did not sit well here.

Under pressure, David blurted out, "Because that would expose the carnality of it."

"The carnality?"

"Yes, then it would look like it was for pleasure."

"Well isn't it?"

"No," David protested, "I have a relationship with the woman, I care. I want her to know."

"That may be true. And the sex may be an expression of it. But it's also for pleasure. Why are you trying to deny that?"

"I'm not trying to deny it. I just . . ."

"You are. You're trying to create an illusion. You're trying to cloak something you think is 'carnal'—in other words, bad—in a particular atmosphere or mind-set. The illusion is broken, intruded on by the condom, which I guess confronts you with: This is clearly for pleasure. You are the acrobat going through your motions, falling in perfect form. What is the illusion? What is it about the stocking that breaks the acrobat's stride?"

David dissociated. He had that otherworldly look of someone who has gone way back in time. What was he thinking? Was he upset? Had I pushed him too hard? I waited patiently until he said, "I'm thinking back to my first sexual experience, which I've told you about. At the lake, on the beach?"

"I remember."

"The guy in the other couple, Mark, was my best friend. He was sexually active before me and very promiscuous. As fond as I was of him, and still am, I didn't want to be that way. I didn't want to just go through women. . . ."

"Because?"

"Where we lived a girl's reputation and desirability were tarnished if she lost her virginity. The same was not true for boys. So the boy, or man, was taking something irrevocable. He was soiling her."

"There was a double standard?"

"A strong one."

"I thought your background was not repressive sexually."

"My parents, my family weren't. As I told you, they weren't very religious. They didn't buy into this double standard."

"But the community was different?"

"In the community there was a strong double standard and still is. It's been watered down a lot in the last generation, but it's still strong and certainly was when I was growing up."

"What kind of Jewish community has a strong double standard?" I asked. "I think of most American Jewish families and communities as not being very repressive and not having a double standard. The small Orthodox community is quite restrictive but, again, it applies the same standard to both sexes."

"Ah," said David. "I'm from neither. My small enclave was Middle Eastern, Sephardic Jews. We all had our roots in predominantly Arab countries: Egypt, Syria, Morocco. We are very different from what you know of European, Ashkenazic Jews."

"Really?"

"That's why my family was different. My parents were more liberal and they valued education, which was unusual. Most Middle Eastern Jews are not highly invested in education and the professions. They're proud of being merchants through and through. They think European Jews are too assimilated."

"And Middle Eastern Jews have a strong double standard?"

"Yes."

To connect this with something I was more familiar with I asked, "Like an Italian, Mediterranean culture?"

"Exactly. Even stronger." David frowned and added, "But I wouldn't have thought it had this kind of effect on me. I didn't think of any of this until a short while ago when you were speculating on the symbolic meaning of a condom to me. These are childhood influences, maybe into early adolescence. I haven't thought of them in years. By college, I was sexually quite active and considered myself not that different from Mark who's mellowed and is still my best friend." David shook his head. "Such a subtle influence."

"You mean not being able to use a condom?"

"Yes."

"It's not just the condom," I said. "The condom is by far the most dramatic piece, but there are other elements as well. In your first sexual experience, the time you went to the beach, you clearly did not want to be like Mark. You had a greater sensitivity to the community's values, the double standard, and the inequity for women. Shortly thereafter you became involved with the Catholic girlfriend, the one with whom you had mutual oral sex. For the remainder of high school, while you were still living in that community, it probably suited you to have a girlfriend who wanted to keep her virginity and to respect that."

"Hmm," said David interrupting me. "I always saw my having a Catholic girlfriend as evidence of how liberal my parents were."

"By college you were sexually active," I continued, "having intercourse with many partners. However, the oral sex was probably a hold over. You said you liked to be *that intimate* before having intercourse. I now think that *intimate* meant you had proven yourself, you were that close and proved you cared that much about the woman, before intercourse. The same was also probably true of your efforts to create the right atmosphere. Again, you were being a gentleman, going out of your way. Of course, all this was quite unconscious on your part and did not detract from your sexual performance. It may have even enhanced it, making you an attentive lover. And it was by no means all bad. Respect for one's partner is very important. But there was a rigidity on your part—the preciousness, the singular concentration—which is the giveaway that more was going on. You were the acrobat, going through your gyrations, proving yourself with a concentrated effort that couldn't be interrupted.

"Enter the condom, the acrobat's stocking, which throws you off balance. It was too close for comfort, too much of an intrusion into your consciousness, signaling just how much your sexual activity was for pleasure. Your concentration is broken and your performance ruined. Not that you knew why, but under these circumstances the conflict overtook you."

David sat intently, taking in all I had said. Then he commented, "It's true. It comes as a surprise but I think this is it.

I can feel it in my gut in a way that I didn't some of the things you suggested earlier. I guess this was the mental block."

"Right."

"But how can I have not known?" David wrestled with the idea.

"It's quite common actually," I responded. "For you this was a blind spot. If you could have seen it you wouldn't have needed to consult me. Inevitably, your blind spot infiltrated our discussion. You described vivid pieces of your sexual history, including the beach scene and acrobat metaphor. We started to put the puzzle together but a key piece was missing. Through our dialogue, our struggle to clarify your conflicts, the crucial piece fell into place and suddenly the whole picture makes sense."

This process was probably slowed a little in David's case because his emotionally charged blind spot coincided with a gap in my knowledge. I had no previous experience with Middle Eastern Jewish culture. Thus it did not occur to me to ask if this was David's background. The limited picture he originally gave of his ethnic and religious background coincided with my expectations of American Jewish communities. Had he said he was Italian, this would have lead to a different line of inquiry on my part. Instead, we went forward unsuspecting and found the clue to his problem via a different angle. This is a small example of what is called a "cross-cultural issue" in psychiatry, when a lack of knowledge about a person's specific culture makes it harder for the therapist to draw out certain details of the patient's history. In spite of this, we were able to get to the bottom of things remarkably quickly, something that rarely happens in just one session.

"Another way to look at your conflict," I said to David, "is as a remnant of an oppressive, in this case religious, background. Outwardly, you long ago began breaking the rules. Inwardly, unconsciously, you were still bargaining with the old order."

David smiled at this, seeming satisfied. Then he asked tongue in cheek, "So, will I be okay tonight?"

We both laughed at his question. We talked about the fact that this might or might not be the cure to his problem. He should probably still tell Laura about his difficulty, soliciting her support and involvement in its solution. If anything sexual happened between them tonight, the goal should simply be their mutual pleasure, not necessarily his maintaining an erection for intercourse with a condom. It was important there be no pressure on him to perform.

David and I scheduled a follow-up appointment in the coming week. He would want to report back in any case and might need to do some more work before the problem was fully resolved.

David returned the next week and excitedly announced "it worked." He successfully had intercourse wearing a condom "on the first try."

"That's wonderful," I said.

"Yes. I was really pleased."

David told Laura the history of his problem and his concern it might recur. She was quite understanding and patient.

"We took things slowly," he said. "We integrated my putting the condom on into our foreplay. We were very relaxed and in the end I had no difficulty."

Indeed, David said he successfully had intercourse several times during the week "just to test the cure."

This kind of quick success is unusual in psychiatry, but

occasionally circumstances are ripe for it. The question that arises in such instances is whether the cure is sustained? David consulted with me a number of years later about an unrelated matter and happily reported his problem wearing condoms had not returned.

DON JUAN'S REGRET

My treatment of Rick was a long and complicated one. A girlfriend of his, Suzanne, was the first to see me. She was finishing a medical residency program and was planning to move home to the Midwest at the time she became involved with Rick. In those days, he was often in relationships with women in transition: finishing school, anticipating a job transfer, or otherwise planning to leave town. He also had a penchant for long-distance relationships. These conflicting circumstances were fertile ground for the confusing signals Rick sent women. He had a long history of stringing women along, giving mixed messages, and being involved in more than one relationship at a time.

"He's a sick Don Juan," Suzanne said one day, referring specifically to Rick's incessant exercising, maintenance of his "beautiful body," which she felt was designed to attract women only to hurt them. Once I met Rick when he came to pick Suzanne up after an appointment. He was, indeed, the epitome of a handsome, well-dressed man. Suzanne was in therapy for six months extricating herself from the relationship with him.

Rick evidently thought I helped Suzanne because in an unusual turn of events, he later referred another girlfriend,

Katie. My opinion of Rick rose immediately; somewhere in him was a humane streak toward women.

Katie moved to Boston because she had been in a long-distance relationship with Rick. Arriving here she found him "radically changed," cold, and distant. After four months of therapy, she decided to return to her job and life in Philadelphia.

At one point, Katie too referred to Rick as a sick Don Juan. Was this a coincidence, I wondered. Or was this a name Rick himself used in pleading his case to women? I was eventually to find out, for to my even greater surprise, a year later Rick called, expressing some urgency, saying, "You helped them. Can you help me?"

Sympathetic to his distressed tone of voice, I made an appointment with Rick for the next day. Greeting him in the waiting room was a shock: Slumped in a chair, unshaven, his clothes hanging off him, he looked a shadow of his former self. "I was head over heels in love with a new girlfriend, Lisa," Rick explained tremulously. "For the first time in my adult life I was monogamous and convinced her to be too. Just when I thought all was going well, about a month ago Lisa began a new affair, cuckolding me. I've been spiraling downwards ever since."

Rick explained he was not sleeping well, his appetite had decreased, and he had lost about ten pounds. An entrepreneur with his own head-hunting firm, he was having difficulty maintaining a minimum standard on the job. Many days he did not even go into work. He was losing touch with friends and not interested in a new relationship. Most noteworthy, from Rick's perspective, he was not working out. "I'm religious about exercising. I have to be feeling really low to give it up."

Rick expressed sadness and dismay that when he was

"finally ready to commit" he should meet with such disappointment. "I should have known. I usually avoid her type because they're dangerous for me. This time I didn't."

"How do you mean *her type*?"

"Petite, ultrathin, flirtatious. . . ." Rick thought a moment then added, "But beneath the surface actually quite strong-willed and independent. I'm irresistibly attracted to women like that. My friends all warned me Lisa was a liability; she was being manipulative and not treating me well. Still, I had trouble seeing it."

"When you say you should have known, has this ever happened to you before?"

Knowing Rick's history of disappointing women, I was a little surprised when he answered, "Yes. Once in high school. I've avoided it since."

The girlfriend in high school had been Rick's first. Before that he had not been attractive to women, "not high on their social list." When a popular, flirtatious girl agreed to date him his senior year, Rick was so elated he "took a lot of shit." She frequently "blew him off," calling just before dates to say something else came up. She also took things from him—records, tapes, sweaters, jackets—and never gave them back. She still had his varsity jacket from playing football in high school. After graduation the girlfriend broke up with him, saying she was moving on to "bigger and better things." Rick was devastated, went off to college depressed, and took almost a year to recover.

"It feels the same now," said Rick. "I'm not over Lisa yet."

In fact, he was besieging Lisa with entreaties to return to him. He barraged her with phone calls, wrote passionate letters, and sent flowers. This is one of the most common symptoms in men who are distraught over a breakup: They dig themselves into a deeper hole with self-defeating attempts to win the girlfriend back. Lisa, too, played a complimentary role. While appearing to disdain Rick's efforts, she gave him mixed messages. For example, about his sending flowers, she said "how sweet" before telling him to "stop doing that." Then, after weeks of insisting Rick stop calling her, Lisa suggested they talk regularly at prearranged times.

The early part of therapy with a man in Rick's condition requires curtailing the self-defeating behavior sufficiently to stabilize the patient and get him back on his feet. Unfortunately, Rick's acting out escalated before it abated. He sent flowers again, annoying Lisa even more. On two occasions he stood across the street from her apartment building to watch her come and go with her new boyfriend. The second time, when they emerged from the building, Rick crossed the street and confronted them. A tense standoff between the two men ensued. Only the fact that the other man was Rick's size made him hesitate to start a fight. Rick said he would like to beat Lisa's boyfriend up. If he saw them again, he was afraid he might "do something stupid."

A few men in Rick's position can be obsessed with the woman for years. They may become assaultive and get hurt in the process. Restraining orders, incarcerations, and involuntary hospitalizations may be the result of this "erotomania." I doubted this would happen with Rick and knew we were a long way from it. However, it was a concern. So I lobbied Rick vigorously that he was being self-defeating: Were his entreaties actually passive-aggressive attempts to annoy Lisa? If, as he alleged, he wanted her back, why was he behaving in a way that might destroy any possibility of a relationship in the future? Might he be giving Lisa what she wanted: two men competing for her with Rick in a compromised position but still waiting in the wings?

After months of such lobbying, Rick finally settled down. He continued to talk with Lisa twice a week but otherwise his efforts stopped. He began renewing other friendships and was functioning better at work. One day Rick appeared with an athletic bag in hand; he was exercising again. Interestingly, with male patients, the appearance of an athletic bag is often an early harbinger of their mood being reliably on the upswing.

One week Rick forgot to telephone Lisa. She immediately contacted him. While Rick was surprised, in my experience this is what usually happens: When the individual dropped in a relationship, whether the man or woman, stops their repeated pleas, the other party almost invariably shows renewed interest.

Now Lisa's ambivalence became more evident as she began to suggest doing things together again. Rick felt incredible relief at seeing Lisa but became increasingly aware how controlling she was. While deferring on most things, Rick balked when she wanted to confide in him about difficulties arising in her affair.

"I don't want to hear about your relationship," he insisted.

"Who else can I talk to?" Lisa pleaded.

"No. I don't want to hear anything until you can tell me it's over."

All the same, Lisa persisted. One morning she appeared on Rick's doorstep in tears after a fight with her boyfriend. Reluctantly, Rick let her in. After they talked a while, she asked him to give her a hug. One thing led to another until Lisa abruptly pushed Rick away. He felt hurt, torn, and confused.

Rick had met his match. Watching him struggle with Lisa was like watching Suzanne and Katie in their earlier struggles with him. The phenomena were two sides of the same coin. What in his background predisposed Rick to his difficulties with women? Why was he vulnerable to such extremes of hurting women or being hurt by them? Why had lasting, committed relationships so far eluded him?

With his depression continuing to improve and his relationship with Lisa on the wane, Rick and I turned our attention to these deeper questions. He started by describing his family history, growing up in a New England town. Rick's parents were married in their early twenties. From a poor background, his father "married up socially." His mother's family openly opposed the marriage, which lasted only three years. Rick and his older sister stayed with their mother whose family supported her modestly. Rick's father remarried and with his new wife raised three stepsons from her former marriage.

Growing up, Rick and his sister felt "caught between two worlds." Among his mother's family they felt like second-class citizens, reminders of his father's brief intrusion. Meanwhile, when they visited their father, Rick and his sister were treated like two "well-mannered, well-bred, rich kids from the other side of town."

"We fit in even less well with them," Rick observed. Rick described an enmeshed, volatile relationship with his mother who was the "domineering influence" in his life. She was an unpredictable woman who often took her temper out on the children. In the heat of the moment, she would tell Rick he reminded her of his father whom she hated.

"Even on good days, when she was being nice, she used to say how much I looked like him which was double-edged. She was wildly attracted to my father, but it resulted in disaster."

On several occasions I asked Rick about his relationship with his father.

"There's much less to say about him," he would respond. "My father's a man's man. He was a construction worker and very macho. He had leathery, weatherbeaten skin and wore lumber jackets and heavy-soled boots. His boots are one of my strongest memories from childhood. They were tall, oversize, and encrusted with dirt and cement."

"Were you close to him?"

Rick shook his head. "No one is. He's the quintessential 'no feelings' guy. His attitude toward life's adversity is 'Suck it up.' His only pleasure in life is sports. That's where we did come together some when I was in high school. He came to my games, and we practiced together."

Whenever I asked Rick about his father, I noticed he would stray back to the topic of his mother.

"She's the one I was closer to and that's the problem. I've been trying to escape her much of my adult life. I think that's what underlies my relationships with women: I can't get close to a woman because every time I do, I feel claustrophobic, like I'm going to be manipulated again. So I flee. At this point I know when I'm attracted to a woman, it's not so much I want her as I want to escape the one I'm with."

While his relationship with Lisa continued to improve, one remnant of Rick's early behavior remained: He kept asking if their romantic relationship could ever be revived. He pressed this in spite of Lisa's repeated rebuffs. Indeed, Rick stepped up his efforts after learning Lisa's affair was "pretty much on the rocks."

"I keep asking her," said Rick, "even though at this point I'm not sure I would want a romantic relationship."

Rick and I looked at this from a number of different angles. Was he angry with Lisa that her affair was a passing thing when it caused him so much pain? Was his solicitousness a passive-aggressive way·of irritating her? Was he being self-destructive, setting himself up to be rejected repeatedly?

I considered Rick's compulsive questioning of Lisa to be important because it was a distillation, the residue of his earlier more floridly disruptive behavior. As such it was potentially telling of whatever Rick was playing out in the relationship and breakup with Lisa. So I kept turning the subject over with him, looking for something new and fruitful. Finally, toward the end of one meeting, I asked him again, perhaps a little impatiently, "Why do you keep pressing, when you know her response is going to be negative?"

"Because I'd rather have a negative response than none at all," said Rick. "What I can't stand is her indifference."

In this statement I heard a larger theme, feelings that went beyond Lisa. This was what I had been looking for. Was Rick referring to his mother? Indifference was not a word he used to describe her attitude toward him.

"What you can't stand is her indifference," I repeated to underscore the feelings.

"Yes."

"Does that remind you of anyone?"

"What do you mean?"

"Not being able to stand someone's indifference. Does that remind you of anybody?"

"My father," Rick blurted out to his dismay.

"Your father."

"Don't ask me what that means!" Rick reared back.

"Any ideas?"

"No. And I don't care to," he said adamantly. Then he laughed, "What was that, a Freudian slip? I don't buy it."

Rick's surprise and his defensive reaction indicated we had stumbled onto something important.

"How could my relationship with my father have anything to do with how I relate to women?" demanded Rick.

"How could it not? At the very least, he was an example of how men relate to women. And his relationship to you could have influenced your relationships with women in other, more subtle ways."

"I don't buy it," Rick reiterated.

Unfortunately, our meeting was over. An old saw in psychotherapy is that patients often blurt out revelations at the end of a meeting because it is safer. While this is usually unconscious, it allows the patient to go away and think about what was said, before having to discuss it.

Rick appeared for our next meeting upset over two dreams he had. Clearly anxious and distracted, he shifted uncomfortably in his chair and repeatedly lost his train of thought trying to reconstruct the dreams. As I listened, I thought Rick was in a predicament: Unwittingly, he was getting into things more deeply than he expected. Said Rick:

> In the first dream I was in a bus with a woman. We were driving up a steep, winding, dirt road, trying to get to the top of a mountain. The bus was overflowing with luggage; suitcases and duffel bags were sticking out the windows and tied on top of the bus. They kept falling off and breaking open, and things rolled all over the ground. I had to get out, stuff them closed, and secure them again.
>
> We were trying to escape being pursued by bandits or hoodlums. Somewhere near the top they caught up with us and there was a terrible shoot-out. Blood was everywhere. I kept picking off my adversaries but more came. One guy popped up a few feet away and I blew his head off at close range. It was sickening.
>
> I told the woman to take cover for her safety. I was con-

cerned because she was the only one without a weapon.
While I was shooting at the men I kept telling her to lie low,
to hide behind the bus or a rock.

At one point the woman—she was my girlfriend but I
can't identify her—came out in the middle of the crossfire. I
yelled at her to protect herself, to protect her heart. When
she didn't get out of the way, I reached over and tore a hubcap off one of the bus's wheels and handed it to her. I told
her to hold the hubcap up to her chest to protect herself. She
needed to be careful she didn't get hit by a bullet, especially
in her heart.

In the middle of the dream, Rick woke up briefly. He
was upset and recalled thinking, "I can't keep doing this to
women. I can't offer them any reasonable protection."
When he lapsed back into the dream, its setting had
changed to an infirmary.

The infirmary was like a makeshift hospital in a war zone. I
was alone in a large room lined with beds. Somehow it was
calm outside and relatively safe. I think we had arrived at the
top of the mountain.

The woman—the same one who'd been driving the bus
and was my girlfriend—came into the room and was now a
nurse. I was wounded from the battle, and she was taking
care of me. I became impatient because she was supposed to
bring me medication but couldn't find it.

Even though I was injured, I had to pull myself out of
bed to go and help her. We went down a long, deserted corri-
dor and eventually came to a room full of giant pills. They
were capsules really; huge phallic things. The nurse had her
arms around one, trying to get it open but couldn't. I got
more and more impatient because I needed the medication.
Also, somehow these huge capsules were the same thing as
the luggage that had fallen off the bus: the suitcases and duffel bags. I don't understand how, but they were the same.

Rick woke from the dream in a sweat. He "couldn't stand the tension" of not being given the medication. Before getting up, he lay in bed for a long time, slowly calming down.

The next night Rick had a second dream, which he thought was related. Some of the themes were similar, even though the settings were quite different. While the first dream was set in a dusty, mountainous terrain, the second was in a modern, urban setting, and Rick was in jail.

I was sitting in a dimly lit cell when I heard footsteps and knew the guard was coming. He was a policeman or soldier in a uniform. After entering the cell, he just stood there. He looked like a fascist, towering over me with his spit-polished, knee-high military boots, his holster, and his gun. He stood with his back to the wall, legs spread apart, arms crossed, and said nothing.

I sat for the longest time afraid and not sure what to do. I considered trying to escape but thought he would stop me. After a while it occurred to me that I should take his gun. I don't know why I thought he wouldn't resist. Reaching up, I lifted his gun out of its holster.

Looking frightened, my jailer stepped back against the wall. I sat pointing the gun at him but felt conflicted. Part of me wanted to kill him. Yet I thought I would never escape; the other guards would surely catch me. Also, I felt sorry for him. He was my jailer but he'd let me take his gun so how could I shoot him? Then I knew what I should do. I'd been pointing it at him but slowly I turned the gun around toward myself and pulled the trigger. Nothing happened! It was a toy gun! I was left shaken and confused.

Then the scene changed. I was no longer in the cell, or even in jail, and the jailer was gone. I was injured and an ambulance had arrived. A woman paramedic who'd driven the ambulance was busy putting me on a stretcher.

Rick stopped, most upset by the final scene in this dream. He was so distressed, I did not push him. Eventually he continued.

> This was the really bizarre part: I was a woman and I was pregnant. The paramedic was telling me to lie on my side on the stretcher because that would be best for the baby. This scene was very tender and moving. The paramedic was bending over, covering me with blankets, and saying everything would be all right. I was overwhelmed with gratitude. I tried to lift myself up a little, straining to give her a kiss. Then I recoiled, saying to myself: "You can't kiss your healer." Again I woke up in a sweat.

Rick kept shaking his head, referring to his dreams as "bizarre." I reassured him that in fact his dreams were not abnormal. They would no doubt prove quite helpful to our work. Rick commented he had a long history of episodic "shoot-'em-up" dreams. He thought both women—the nurse/bus driver and paramedic—were girlfriends but could not identify them. Both dreams were set against a backdrop in which a struggle or battle was going on: the shoot-out in one, incarceration in the other. But beyond these basic comparisons, he had no idea what the dreams meant. As the session ended, we agreed to discuss the dreams in more depth the following week.

The day before our next appointment Rick called to cancel. He left a message saying he was stopping therapy because he was feeling much better, things with Lisa were under control, and he no longer felt he needed it.

In his message, Rick obviously sidestepped the emotional issues coming up in therapy. I called him back to say we should meet to discuss his stopping but he refused. I tried a few angles, saying this was no way to finish our work, but Rick was adamant. At that point my goals for the telephone conversation changed. I wanted to give Rick some handle on what was happening and leave the door open. I told him I thought therapy was getting into emotions that were uncomfortable for him. The slip about his father and the two dreams indicated things were coming to the surface that he was having trouble dealing with. If he changed his mind, at any point in the future, he could always return. He was not burning his bridges; it was all right for him to take a break.

Patients almost always need to take breaks from therapy. Most of them can do so without actually leaving. When things get too intense, they simply back off and talk about more superficial things. When ready, they return to the difficult material.

For whatever reasons Rick needed literally to leave therapy. Of course, there was the chance he might not come back, but I would have been surprised. One can usually rely on a patient's symptomatology to return if the underlying issues have not been dealt with sufficiently. In Rick's case his symptoms were his tortured relationships with women and his resulting dysphoria.

Rick's dreams had, in fact, been about his therapy. It was true the women in the dreams were girlfriends, caught in Rick's struggles. But the two women also symbolized me. The most obvious clue was that they were health professionals, a nurse and paramedic. The dreams occurred after Rick's Freudian slip about his father. For some patients such slips are frightening windows into worlds they would rather not know. What kind of journey (the bus and ambulance) was Rick being taken on in therapy? Who was in control

(Who was driving?) and was he comfortable with that? Did his care giver have the medication he needed (the nurse who could not open the oversize pills)?

Most important was the closing scene of the second dream, in which Rick said to himself: "You can't kiss your healer." This scene poignantly represented his desire on the one hand to get close to me, to have someone treat his pain, and on the other hand his enormous fears. What emotions was he pregnant with but afraid of in therapy?

Therapy will always be an art and not a science. The decision on how to respond to Rick's bolting was a crucial one, instinctual on my part. My decision to let Rick go was made in a matter of minutes, in response to his psychological stance and tone of voice. Should I have pressed him more to come back? Perhaps, but I thought not. Pressuring him could be counterproductive, strengthening his defenses against therapy, and lessening the likelihood he would return.

While working with someone, I always have a list of unanswered questions in the back of my mind. In Rick's case the list had grown quite long. One minor, obscure, but potentially important point was: When describing his ill-fated relationship as a senior in high school, Rick said this was the first time he had been attractive to women. Why had he not been attractive to them before? What was the history there?

In a similar vein: What was the significance of his physical attraction to petite, thin women, and his own compulsive working out?

On a larger scale, the question of what Rick was acting out with women had not been answered. What was the role of his father in all of this? Were questions of sexual identity at the bottom of Rick's problems? Folk wisdom has it that, in some instances, Don Juans are running from homosexual impulses. This might be the case or it could be an oversimplification.

Finally, what was the meaning of Rick's potent dreams? They rose up in the therapy like hieroglyphic tablets waiting to be deciphered. What was the significance of Rick's history of intermittent shoot-'em-up dreams? How did women get caught in the crossfire? Why the male/female transpositions?

Some six months later Rick returned to therapy. He had begun a new relationship the month before and his day-to-day anxiety level rose dramatically. Distracted, he became less productive.

"I wasn't in a relationship for five months after I last saw you," said Rick. "That's the longest I've gone since college. In fact, as you know, I'm usually in more than one relationship at a time. It felt good to be able to go without a girlfriend. I felt stable. Then I began dating this woman, Sally. Because I had a girlfriend, all sorts of things started to happen again. Since therapy, I'm more conscious of my problems with women. Even though I can't stop myself, I'm uncomfortable."

Rick explained his new relationship quickly became sexual. He was making an effort not to lead Sally on, but knew she was developing expectations and would be hurt. Since seeing Sally, he had also had sex a few times with a consultant at work, a woman he did not really like or respect. Rick was "seduced" by the woman's lavish praise of his body, which he "could not resist." Being even more honest, Rick said this "sleazy affair was an escape hatch" necessitated by being in the relationship with Sally. In addition, Lisa had reappeared, "begging" him to get back together once she discovered he was dating other women.

Rick described this cascade of events with a confessional tone. He felt guilty and self-reproachful.

"Does it make sense to you," he asked, "that all this would happen and I'd become anxious since getting into a relationship?"

"Yes," I responded. "I can understand why you would have felt more even-keeled without one. It's like abstinence, or being sober, for a while. For you, getting back into a relationship is like returning to a drug habit."

"Exactly," said Rick with a mixture of relief and embarrassment. "You know the AA slogan: You can't have just one drink? That's what it's like. I'm right back on the same merry-go-round. At this point, I want to change."

I noted Rick was more open, more accessible. His motivation for coming into therapy was more balanced. The last time around he sought therapy in the throes of a crisis. This time he returned because of anxiety, self-reflection, and a desire to change. He also seemed less of a cardboard figure now than when I first met him. More in touch with his emotions, he had more depth.

Over the next several months, Rick examined his relationship with Sally. While enjoying her company, he was convinced he would not be interested in a lifelong commitment with her. During this time he had several more rendezvous in his "sleazy affair" with the consultant, his escape from the relationship with Sally. Eventually he "got up the courage to be really honest" with Sally and break off their relationship. She was upset and wanted to continue "even if Rick was not 100 percent into it." Rick held his ground although this was difficult for him to do. This was the first time he had ever broken up with a woman instead of mistreating her until she left him.

A few weeks later, Rick announced a new goal for himself: The next time he began seeing someone he was going to ask the difficult question of whether or not he was genuinely interested in the woman before their relationship became sexual.

"The fact that my relationships become sexual so quickly," observed Rick, "complicates things. No matter how liberated people are, sex creates a whole set of expectations."

"How quickly do they become sexual?" I asked.

"Usually in a matter of days, by the second date. A lot of the women I go out with I've known for some time, socially or through work. But once romantic involvement is an acknowledged possibility, things move quickly. Days. A week at most."

"Why do you move so quickly?"

"I don't know." Rick pondered the question. "Without the sex I feel restless."

"Restless?"

"Yes. In a sexual relationship I'm proving myself to a woman. Once sex has entered the realm of possibility, I'm impatient for it to happen. The only time I'm not forthcoming and impulsive sexually is much later in a relationship: I sometimes withdraw sexually from a woman if all else fails."

"What do you mean *if all else fails*?"

"Usually I let women down on the commitment end of things: not being able to get close, being involved in other relationships, and so on. Occasionally, I meet a woman who doesn't mind. She's a free spirit, and it's okay with her. I guess I'm uncomfortable under those circumstances. I've noticed I withdraw sexually. I become apathetic. I'm no longer passionate, sexually, about the relationship."

"And what happens?"

"That usually confuses the woman, who drifts away."

"You've finally found a level on which to disappoint her."

Rick nodded, intrigued by this formulation. "But it's a last resort. I try to fail women at every other level first."

"Why do you think your sexual prowess is more important to you than anything else in a relationship?"

Rick shrugged.

"Maybe proving myself physically? A need to know women find me attractive and satisfying."

Thereafter Rick worked diligently on holding back sexually when he became involved with women. The first few times he tried this he was surprised by how insecure he felt. He realized he had been using sex as a form of premature closure to avoid the emotional aspects of intimacy, which were more difficult for him.

The other side of Rick's habitual seductive behavior was being revealed in therapy. Beneath its surface we were discovering his insecurities and low self-esteem, his desperate need for reassurance from women, and his repeated failure to achieve this because of the throwaway nature of his relationships. Slowly, we were getting into Rick's pain.

In one meeting, which proved to be a turning point, I asked, "You once said you weren't attractive to women before your junior and senior years in high school. Why was that the case?"

"That's a part of my history I'd rather forget."

"Oh?"

"It gets into my relationship with my father too."

Here my interest was piqued. At the same time I wanted to proceed slowly, because this subject made Rick bolt from therapy once before.

"Can you tell me a little about it?" I asked cautiously.

Grimacing, Rick explained he was a late bloomer physically. "When I was young I was a short, scrawny, awkward kid. In grade school and junior high I was teased and picked on a lot."

Rick stopped. Like most men who begin to relate this type of history, he did not volunteer details. However, the details are important because otherwise one is skirting the issue.

"What did they say or do?" I asked.

"They called me a sissy, a faggot," said Rick, a little red faced. "They pushed my books out of my hands. They stole my lunch box. It was all kid stuff, but it's brutal when you're young. My tormentor in grade school was Nicky Strom. He headed a gang of boys who were always ambushing and beating me up."

I thought of Rick's dreams. Tormentor . . . jailer. Ambush . . . shoot-'em-up.

By late grammar school, said Rick, most of the boys in his class were on athletic teams. He repeatedly tried but never made the teams. By junior high, the tormenting became worse. "I can recall vividly the locker room in junior high school, because I was teased so ruthlessly there. Once when I had just gotten dressed, another boy told me to leave the locker room because I didn't belong, I was such a wimp. For some reason I answered him back. I said no, I belonged as much as he did, which was ludicrous. He was an overdeveloped jock. He started pushing me toward the door and I don't know what came over me. I must have been blinded by hurt and rage. I started swinging at him even though it was ridiculous. He was at the front of a pack of about six boys. He picked me up, threw me against a bank of lockers, and started strangling me with his hands. I was panic-stricken, becoming short of breath. He might have choked me if the other boys hadn't pulled him off.

They left me in a heap on the floor and ran out of the locker room laughing. Talking about it, their laughter still reverberates in my head."

Rick had many such stories, which are not uncommon. Boys are often tormented in this way. The experience is usually merciless and leaves deep psychological scars.

It all changed, Rick said, in high school. He had a tremendous growth spurt, shooting up in height and gaining weight. All of a sudden, coaches were interested in him. When he was recruited onto the football team he was elated. "I had to work hard to catch up, but I gradually worked my way onto the first-string team. That's when I suddenly became popular with the girls. I was this dark horse who'd slowly moved into the lead. Still, I wasn't prepared for it. It didn't seem real to me. That's why I put up with so much shit from the girlfriend my senior year, the one who never returned my varsity jacket."

I nodded. The pieces were finally coming together.

In college, it took Rick a long time to accept the idea he was attractive to women. "It was unreal to go to parties or bars and have women hit on me," he said.

Rick's later athletic prowess and physique certainly camouflaged his earlier history. However, this early history was crucial, helping to explain his extreme emphasis on physical appearance, his compulsive exercising, and his need to prove himself sexually with women. Still, I felt something was missing. Why hadn't Rick felt better about himself before he was an athlete? Why hadn't becoming one been more of a cure for his insecurities? Why was he so often limited in his relationships, incapable of going beyond superficial, sexualized, interpersonal fixes?

In one of our meetings, I asked, "You said this history

would lead into the relationship with your father, yet you haven't mentioned him again."

"I have an even harder time dealing with his part in it."

"His part in it?"

"Yes," said Rick reluctantly. "As I told you, my father's very masculine. He's very impatient with anything short of that. He was a construction worker and a sports fan. All the years I was scrawny and incompetent athletically he didn't know what to do with me. He couldn't relate."

Although Rick had told me his father was a construction worker, macho, and followed sports, now this had greater meaning. I recalled his father's oversize boots, one of Rick's "strongest memories" from his childhood. Then I thought again of Rick's dreams: the jailer in the knee-high military boots.

"My father was a difficult man to learn anything from," Rick explained haltingly. "Very impatient. I remember once when I was a kid he was teaching me to swim underwater. He ran out of patience fairly quickly and simply ordered me to swim the length of the pool without coming up for air. When I hesitated, petrified, he pointed to the far end of the pool and shouted, 'Swim, goddamn it!' As I swam, I could see him pacing alongside, looking on. The last half of the pool my lungs were bursting; I thought I might suffocate. But his words were so forceful, I probably would have drowned rather than come up for air."

Suffocating underwater with his father looking on, I tried to imagine. Then I remembered Rick short of breath with Nicky Strom strangling him in the locker room. No doubt in Rick's unconscious the two were blurred: oppressive men trying to squeeze the life out of him because he did not measure up to their standards.

Rick's difficulties with his father were compounded by the contrast between Rick's lack of athletic ability and the athletic skills of his father's stepsons.

"Their house was full of sports equipment, a game was always on television, they talked endlessly about teams, trades, and scores. I felt like the sissy, the runt, the odd man out."

"What about in high school?" I asked. "You once said your father took an interest in you athletically in high school. By then you were more accomplished."

"He did. He made an effort. But I never felt he was impressed. My stepbrothers played football for years before I did. I never became as good as they were. Even when I made first string, it was another story of their side of town versus ours. They went to a rougher high school with a much better football team. Every year we played them and got creamed. I never felt I measured up in my father's eyes."

"Never measured up athletically?"

"Which was his definition of masculinity. I perpetually felt inadequate."

"It's unfortunate you've incorporated his standards given their affect on you."

"I always thought he cared more for his stepsons. I thought I must really be a disappointment for him not to prefer me."

I thought Rick was taking too much of the blame for the failure of his relationship with his father. I brought this up gently by saying, "You had a lot of other qualities he might have appreciated but it seems he didn't."

"I tried. Even in high school, when I was doing well athletically but still felt I was letting him down, I tried to have a relationship that went beyond sports. For example, I made an effort to involve him in my decisions about colleges. But I failed; I couldn't get him interested."

"Listen to yourself: You 'failed,'" I said to Rick. "Did he make any effort?"

"No. He would just go blank when I mentioned colleges or careers. You know what his response was when I got into college? 'Where will you get the money?' That's all. No congratulations. Nothing."

Rick was frequently agitated and at times expressed regret, disappointment, sadness, and anger when discussing his history with his father. These sessions were emotionally tense, significantly more so than when discussing his mother or even his tormenters at school. No doubt his mother and the school stories were volunteered first precisely because they were less charged. Rick's unresolved issues lay squarely with his father.

As in Rick's case, it often takes a long time in therapy to develop the trust to expose such painful depths. People who wall off parts of their history do so for a reason: the associated emotions are intolerable. This changes only slowly. Now I was hearing what I sometimes call the "revisionist history": the same dates and events, this time with the crucial painful details included. It takes courage to delve into this kind of material.

One day Rick came to therapy upset over a childhood memory. The memory was what is called a "screen memory": a daydreamlike recollection of the past, an emotionally charged cameo laden with psychological meaning.

I was staying at my father's house. He was a foreman by then and extremely conscientious about his work. It was early November and cold, but there hadn't been any snowfall yet. He was working on the early stages of a construction site. This particular night he and his crew left a lot of cinder blocks out around the foundation so they could start right to work in the morning.

That night it rained, which my father hadn't expected. Then, at around midnight, the temperature went below freezing. My father woke me to say he was going to work and needed my help. I dressed with that eerie feeling one has after being woken up in the black of night. We drove to the construction site, which was an hour away.

Approaching the floodlit site in the middle of a cold winter night was awe inspiring. Everything was covered with ice. My father took out a huge blow torch and began melting the ice off the cinder blocks. As they thawed, I carried them one at a time, putting them under cover so his crew could begin working with them first thing in the morning. We toiled for three hours, into the early morning, in the freezing cold. We hardly spoke, just working steadily, nonstop.

It was exhilarating. On the way home, sitting beside my father in the car, I felt wonderful. We didn't say a word but there was this unspoken acknowledgment of a job well done. I remember being afraid to speak for fear of breaking the spell. That's just about the only time I remember feeling close to my dad. The rest of the time, in his house, I felt he and my stepbrothers were playing by a set of rules I didn't understand and couldn't measure up to.

Here, for the first time in therapy, Rick began to cry. His crying was heartfelt and cathartic. We had reached his emotional bedrock. Through his tears Rick said he spoke with one of his stepbrothers during the week and told him the memory. The stepbrother said he too went along that night to help. Rick had no recollection of his stepbrother's presence, so strong was his desire to have his father's undivided attention.

How poignant, I said, that this was Rick's only memory of closeness with his father. Even in this moment of glory he had to rely on projection, on an "unspoken acknowledgment" of a job well done. Moreover, this treasured scene was colored by fear: Rick's fear that his speaking up might break the spell. How telling that in the memory he obliterated the rival stepbrother who, apart from this one snapshot, was the uncontested winner in a game Rick felt ill-equipped to play.

This memory and Rick's emotional reaction to it were a turning point. Over the following months he continued to discuss his relationship with his father and his relationships with women. Gradually, it became clear he was talking about the same thing: proving himself physically and feeling inadequate and insecure, needy and dependent, angry and vengeful. This is an exhilarating stage in therapy when one can overlay the present problem on its underlying dynamic from the past. One day, for example, Rick was talking about his anger and resentment toward women.

"In a lot of ways I resent women for judging men so superficially. It angered me in high school that I was suddenly attractive because my biceps had developed. I was still the same person."

"But you play into it," I said, "with your working out and emphasis on appearance."

"I know, but that's my insecurities. When you've been burned as badly as I was, you can't help yourself. If you find a way to make things work better you can't resist. But you can still resent the whole basic premise. I didn't trust the game even as I became addicted to it."

"Didn't the pattern of being valued on the basis of your physical prowess begin with your father?" I ventured, shifting to the underlying issue.

"I'm sick of performing for women," Rick replied, ignoring my comment.

"What you're really talking about is being sick of performing for your father. Surely any number of the women you've dated would have accepted you if only you were ready. It's the relationship with your father you keep repeating."

Thereafter Rick and I moved more fluidly between the present and past, women and his father. Never feeling masculine enough in his father's eyes, Rick turned to women for validation of his masculinity. Because physical prowess was the dimension on which he had failed, he was the most consistent about proving himself physically with women. But with his low self-esteem and impulse to repeat the father-son legacy, his relationships were doomed to fail. Convinced he was not worthy of another's love, he went around spurning before he was spurned, rejecting in anticipation of being rejected. The unresolved issues with his father left him feeling needy and dependent on women. But his dependence was hostile.

Rick and I spent many sessions going over his hieroglyphic dreams. In the first, he and a woman attempt to escape a group of hoodlums and bandits. His pursuers represent his struggle in the world of men: the tormenting schoolboys, the rival stepbrothers, and ultimately, his father. The bus Rick and the woman drive in is full of luggage: suitcases and duffel bags that keep falling onto the road, spilling their contents. Rick's having to repack and resecure the luggage hinders the couple's progress. This burden represents Rick's old baggage, the issue of his masculinity. The sausage-shaped duffel bags, sticking out the windows of the bus and draped on its roof, would later "somehow be the same thing" as the phallic pills.

When Rick and the woman are overtaken by his nemesis a shoot-out occurs. Now it is clear how women get caught in the crossfire of his struggles in the world of men. He worries because the woman is "the only one without a weapon." He tells her to protect herself, especially her heart. How many women ended up with broken hearts in the carnage of his battles? He lamely reaches for a hubcap from the bus and offers it to his companion to protect herself. Then he awakens with the thought: "I can't keep doing this to women. I can't offer them any reasonable protection."

Later, in the hospital, Rick becomes impatient because the woman, now a nurse, cannot find the medicine he needs. The two go searching and find the giant pills, the phallic symbols of what he wants from women. In his dream the woman cannot open the medication. Deep within him is the conviction his relationships with women are doomed and he awakens in frustration.

In the second dream, he is imprisoned by a jailer, the towering figure in boots who represents his father. His physical appearance—uniform, holster, and gun—declare his unequivocal masculinity and dominance. After a while, Rick reaches up and takes the father's gun from its holster. Here Rick attempts to usurp his father, to take his birthright. He points the gun at his father, but cannot bring himself to pull the trigger. Excruciatingly conflicted in his anger at his father, Rick turns the anger against himself, retroflexes the gun, and pulls the trigger. To his horror and dismay it is a toy. What is the limited nature of his father's strength? Where can Rick turn for relief from his misery?

Wounded, Rick is met by a woman paramedic in an ambulance. The woman healer, symbolic of me, is sympathetic and reassuring. Himself now a woman, Rick is pregnant with the possibility of change. Lying on a stretcher, he reaches forward desperate for treatment and overcome with gratitude but recoils with the thought: "You can't kiss your healer." The male/female transpositions are present because they are basic to his psychopathology: transposing the relationship with his father into his relationships with women, turning to women for validation of his masculinity, now looking for the same from me. Even he has become a woman in his quest for validation. In his mind, where in the world of men would he ever find it?

The imagery in Rick's dreams provided an opportunity to discuss the issue of whether or not he had ever had questions about his sexual identity. The gender transpositions and particularly the scenes in which he lifts his father's gun from its holster and wants to kiss his healer might be construed as homosexual. As we discussed this, I asked, "Some men with your history—feeling inadequate physically, being teased, having been called a sissy—will have questions at one point or another about their sexual orientation. Have you?"

Rick responded that he had had no homosexual experience, fantasies, or dreams. He acknowledged difficulty getting close to men because of his early history, but it had never translated into a desire for physical intimacy to bridge that gap. On the basis of our discussions I concluded these scenes in Rick's dreams were not sexual in nature but simply symbolic of his struggle for personal validation and intimacy with men and women.

Rick was surprised to find the relationship with his father to be the culprit in his relationships with women. He commented, "Remember I thought it was my unfinished business with my mother?"

"Yes."

In an ironic, humorous tone Rick said, "I thought it was their mothers men were looking for in girlfriends."

That is certainly the popular notion, I explained. But in reality psychodynamics—what drives one's behavior—are not gender specific. Men can take their issues with their fathers and act them out with women. Many women gravitate to men who are like their mothers.

"Could I have worked these issues out with a woman therapist?" Rick asked one day.

"Oh, absolutely," I said. "Let's not get into another sexist trap."

Rick laughed.

I added, "Your struggle with a woman therapist would have been different. The therapy would have been stuck for a long time in your trying to seduce her like any other woman. But then our work was characterized by fits and starts for a long time too, only for different reasons."

Rick was in therapy for a number of years. As his therapy progressed he occasionally slipped back into old transference issues, treating or expecting me to be like his father. A few times, as Rick became increasingly emotional, he moved too quickly and became overwhelmed. He would blame me, briefly feeling my support for his wading into deeper emotional waters was like his father saying, "Swim, goddamn it!" With our openness and rapport we were able to work through such distortions.

Over time, Rick's relationships with women gradually improved. He went through a series of monogamous relationships. The monogamy itself was substantial progress. Each of the relationships was transitional in his movement toward an increasingly healthy, committed relationship. Working on his own emotional development, Rick became more competent at the nonsexual aspects of relationships and less dependent on proving himself physically with women.

Rick's relationship with his mother improved dramatically. Relieved of the pressure he had been putting on their relationship, blaming it for his difficulties with women, the air cleared between them. In spite of their difficulties, Rick had always been fond of his mother and the strength she showed raising two children on her own.

While in therapy, Rick made several trips to visit his father. Observing him, Rick became aware that his father's impatience and rigidity were not limited to the world of athletics. In almost all areas he was contentious, emotionally immature, and "could never be wrong."

During one visit, Rick asked if he could borrow his father's car to see a friend. Because his father was not going out that evening, Rick was dismayed when he balked. The father's wife became aware of the situation and said, "Rick, don't you know your father by now? He wants to argue over it with you. If you just put up a fight, he'll let you have the car. That's all it would take."

"I didn't want to fight with him over the car," said Rick in therapy. "I'm tired of relating to him that way. I want something different."

Over time, Rick realized his father was not going to change and worked out a new way of relating to him. For later visits, for example, Rick simply rented a car. Taking a more objective view of his father and working around his limitations, Rick's relationship with him actually improved. One often sees this in therapy: After going through a phase in which the relationship with a parent deteriorates, in the end the relationship is better than it was originally.

An important theme in the closing phase of Rick's therapy was an issue he referred to as, "What the hell is the nature of masculinity?" Rick struggled with what had been his father's definition of masculinity, his "suck it up" attitude toward adversity, and his emotional stuntedness. As Rick noted, this was reinforced by much of the culture at large.

"Sometimes I feel like I was just born at the wrong time," Rick said. "Twenty years earlier and I'd have been a 1950s man, more comfortable in a macho skin. Twenty years later and I'd have been more comfortable with the changing expectations of men. I got caught in the middle: a Don Juan, but not without regret."

In his ferment Rick was struggling, as many men are today, to redefine masculinity in a postfrontier society and in the wake of the feminist movement. Gradually, over time, he developed what he called "an alternative definition of masculinity," which balanced physical strength with psychological strength, maturity, and responsibility. Rick continued to work out and be invested in his athletic well-being. However, in his words, he shed the former "desperate quality of his fixation on physical prowess."

In our closing months, Rick brought the woman he would later marry with him to therapy a number of times. Interestingly, she identified the same issues and vulnerabilities in Rick and was taking much the same stance encouraging his emotional growth, as I was in therapy.

After Rick left therapy he came back to see me briefly when he and his wife were pregnant with their first child. He came in because of his anxieties in general about becoming a father and specifically his fear of having a son. He feared a reawakening of the competitive issues in the relationship with his father.

In fact, Rick and his wife had a daughter and were quite happy. As he left therapy again, shortly after his daughter's birth, he said of fathering a son, "I haven't had to deal with that one yet."

SEXUAL APPETITES

Melanie was an attractive, if hesitant, blue-eyed, blond young woman with an eating disorder. Although she described herself as overweight, most people would not. She had a large frame but was trim and healthy looking. Since early in high school she had had a problem with binging on junk food, then vomiting it up to avoid weight gain. Like most women suffering from bulimia, Melanie was mortally embarrassed telling me about her habit. She had never volunteered this information to anyone before. Only her mother and a few of her friends "guessed" from her behavior.

Melanie was a freshman at Harvard College when she first came to see me because her eating disorder was worsening. Her binging and purging were increasing in frequency and, for the first time, she was losing weight. She was concerned the eating disorder was "taking over her life" and was worried that she might become anorexic.

Like many people today, Melanie lacked a strong sense of self. Describing herself as "directionless," Melanie said she had no goals in life except those that others "fed" her. She had always been a high achiever academically and also excelled in a number of extracurricular activities. She was valedictorian of her high school class, a National Merit

Scholar, and a performer of modern dance. But Melanie felt like a "puppet," "an empty shell," someone who merely complied with the expectations others had for her. Away from home for the first time, she felt "rudderless." Her mother, in particular, had always structured her life, keeping her schedule, chauffeuring her around, editing her papers, and picking out all her clothes. She was angry with herself for being less functional in the absence of such close attention.

"I'm afraid I'm going to fail," said Melanie tearfully. "I'm going to flunk out and disappoint everyone."

At college, Melanie feared her grades might suffer from her feeling bereft and being preoccupied with food. A perfectionist, she was seriously considering dropping out of school before her grades were affected.

I encouraged Melanie to defer this decision. Dropping out and returning home would most likely be an overreaction to her current circumstances. I suggested earning less than straight A's might not be such a terrible thing. Perhaps there had been too great an emphasis on grades in her past. There might be more important developmental tasks for her to accomplish this semester and year.

Because repeated vomiting, if frequent enough, can be life-threatening, I asked Melanie to see an internist for a check up and laboratory tests, which she agreed to. All her tests came back normal, confirming my impression that while Melanie's bulimia was certainly worrisome, she was not in danger.

From the beginning of our work, I was struck by Melanie's hesitancy and indecisiveness. She had difficulty asserting herself with friends, teachers, and other people. If friends asked her to join them socially, she was unable to say no, even if she preferred to stay home and study. Recognizing she was a talented student, one of her professors asked her to be a research assistant. Even though she did not like the professor or the subject matter, Melanie could not think of a gracious way to decline.

"Basically," she said, "if someone asks me to do something, I always think I should. I feel too guilty to say no."

As a result, Melanie quickly found herself overcommitted to extracurricular activities, the research assistant position, and socializing with friends. This was a large part of her frustration and concern about her studies. Moreover, this frustration was a cause of her increased binging and purging.

Melanie said things had not gotten out of hand like this in high school because her life was so much more structured. However, she noted she had always been compliant with boyfriends who typically dominated her. When in a relationship, she would follow a boyfriend's lead, doing what interested him. She had a number of boyfriends in high school, including one or two she did not even really like, but she had been unable to resist their "intense attention." As part of this discussion, Melanie mentioned she would often sleep with boyfriends before she was ready or wanted to.

"Were you ever coerced?" I asked concerned.

"No, no, never. It's just that in general, my boyfriends, rather than I, decided when we were going to sleep together."

Despite her reservations about being dominated, being in a relationship was important to Melanie. She had not yet found a boyfriend in college and was hoping to before long.

Melanie required considerable support and encouragement for curtailing some of the extracurricular activities she was less interested in. She wanted to "get back to basics," focusing on her studies and just a few outside interests. While supporting her cutting back, I was glad Melanie wanted to keep a few activities other than her studies because I suspected academic pursuits had been overemphasized in her life.

Encouraging someone to set limits and be more self-assertive requires going over their interactions with other people in minute detail. We regularly dissected Melanie's exchanges with others, looking for places she might have asserted herself and hypothesizing how she could do so in the future. This is a slow, watchful process, literally drawing out and encouraging a nascent self. Slowly, Melanie began to report examples of when she had, at least to some degree, set and accomplished her own goals.

At the same time, we discussed Melanie's background, looking for the origin of her difficulties. She was from a comfortably well-off, upper-middle-class family. She described her parents, particularly her mother, as extremely conscious of appearances, achievement, and status. Adolescents with eating disorders almost always come from such backgrounds.

Melanie said her mother was the "central figure" in her life. Describing her mother, she used words like *unhappy, unfulfilled, intense,* and *domineering.* Her mother raised three children, Melanie and two older brothers. Now in law school, her eldest brother was quite successful academically as well as athletically. He was the parents' favorite of the two boys. Becoming a lawyer, or another professional, was "just right" in their eyes. They had difficulty with the middle child who was more artistically inclined. The parents had had "many a battle" with the younger brother, whom Melanie "felt sorry for." He was "really going against the tide," declining to be in a preprofessional track in college.

Regarding herself, Melanie said her mother had "something of a double standard." She was more restrictive with Melanie than she had been with her sons. The mother did not "run their lives," the way she had Melanie's.

"Maybe it was her experience with my younger brother and not wanting to have the same thing happen with me. Maybe it was because I was the only girl. Sometimes I think she's lived vicariously through my achievements."

Once Melanie reached high school age, her mother embarked on a series of unsatisfying minicareers: teaching exercise, then yoga, and now dance. At one point, she tried to return to school to finish her own college education, but failed.

"What happened?" I asked, cognizant of Melanie's own thoughts of dropping out of college.

"I'm not really sure. She took a few courses, then didn't complete one and stopped altogether. I think she had trouble with math and science requirements and decided she just couldn't do it. She gave up."

Extremely thin and attractive in appearance, Melanie's mother was "obsessed" with nutrition, calories, diet, and weight. She followed various food fads, being macrobiotic and vegetarian at different times.

From early on, Melanie's weight had been an issue between them. Melanie's body build came more from her father's side of the family, which had a larger bone structure. She could never be as thin as her mother wanted. She was only ten years old when her mother first put her on a diet to lose her prepubescent fat and gain a more idealized figure.

Melanie described her mother's personality as rigid and controlling: If anyone put something in the dishwasher the wrong way, her mother would take everything out and repack it. No matter how clean one left the food processor, it was never good enough. Her mother always took it apart again and scoured it.

I had a growing sense of Melanie's frustrated mother, unsatisfied in her own educational and career goals, burying herself in obsessional tasks, and also of Melanie, the prized daughter whom the mother supported, encouraged, and lived through vicariously. Meanwhile, Melanie herself felt "empty" and like "a puppet on a string" and had difficulty functioning on her own. Melanie told me two stories in particular that epitomized this mother-daughter relationship.

In the first, Melanie said she never picked out her own clothes; her mother chose them all for her. She recalled the last time she indicated an interest in a dress. When Melanie emerged from the dressing room with it on, her mother announced within earshot of the other customers and sales staff: "Your breasts look too big in that. You look cheap." The experience was humiliating.

In the second story, when Melanie was seven years old her mother scrapped all the furniture in her room, even though Melanie was quite attached to it. Her mother said Melanie was now "old enough to take care of a good bedroom set." She stripped the room to the bare walls and redecorated it lavishly in girlish pinks and whites, with imitation French provincial furniture including a four-poster bed. Thereafter Melanie could not hang her own artwork or pictures on her bedroom walls because they "spoiled" the decor. In spite of her protests, Melanie was only allowed to hang things on the back of the bedroom door.

These images—Melanie humiliated in the dress she chose, and her sterile, lavishly decorated bedroom—often came back to me as we worked together. They captured the combination of material comforts and psychological constraints that characterized her life. Episodes like these had drained the will out of her. She became a shell of a person, a superb performer with no sense of self-determination. I saw Melanie as a young girl trapped in the opulent bedroom where her personal initiative was confined to the rear of the door.

Melanie said her response to all this had been to acquiesce, to conform to her mother's wishes, to keep the peace.

"I've never stepped outside the relationship and looked at it quite so starkly before. I couldn't have; I was too dependent on her. I guess being separated from my mother, coming to college, has forced the issue."

Melanie described her father as a businessman who was only modestly successful. He inherited a company from his father who built it from nothing and then turned it over to his son. Melanie's father kept the business running smoothly but failed to expand it. While supporting his family comfortably, he was disappointed with his lackluster career. Her mother often belittled him. Melanie clearly felt solicitous and protective toward him.

Because of the nature of her relationship with her mother, Melanie never had an adolescent rebellion. On second thought, she commented, "Except for my bulimia. She never approved of that. It really upset her. But I felt my body and what I put into it were the only thing I had control over."

This led into the subject of Melanie's eating disorder and its position in the contest of wills between mother and daughter. Since our initial meeting, I had steered clear of her bulimia. By contrast many modern treatment approaches would have focused on it with food charts and food diaries. Unless the condition is life-threatening, such a focus is better avoided because it runs the risk of replicating the intrusive relationship with the parent, which is invariably present. I prefer to work on the underlying issues first. Once a trusting relationship is established, the patient will bring up the eating disorder and a desire to change. The patient's taking the initiative is vitally important because autonomy is so central a theme.

Melanie's first comment on her eating disorder was that food was a source of nourishment and consolation, a soothing area of her life that she felt she could control. "I binge when I'm upset for one reason or another," she said. "I use food to comfort myself. Sometimes it's a reward. If I'm having a difficult day, I tell myself, 'When you get home, you can eat.'"

Many women describe such a relationship to food but in eating disorders this reaches an extreme. (This is also true, of course, for the small number of men who suffer from eating disorders.) The whole issue of control in eating disorders is paradoxical. On the one hand, Melanie felt in control of how much food, a source of nourishment and comfort, she put into herself. Moreover, purging allowed her to eat as much as she wanted without weight gain. However, this form of control is illusory and typical of addictive behaviors. Melanie was only in control of the food per se. The food could not resist her; she decided how much of it to take in. But her eating behavior, her psychological appetite, was completely out of control, dangerous, and self-abusive.

As part of our discussions, I encouraged Melanie to take note of what feelings were associated with the urge to binge. Her first observation was that she often binged late at night, when she was alone. "A binge gives me something to do," she noted. "I don't feel so lonely. After taking that much in, I don't feel so sad."

"Where do you get the food, late at night?"

"If it's before midnight, I'll go to the local twenty-four-hour store. If it's later and I don't feel safe, I . . ." Melanie paused, embarrassed, then said, "I go down to the basement of the dorm and raid the vending machines. I'm not the only one; I see a lot of other girls there for the same reason. If you go too late, the machines are empty."

This was a window into the desperation that women like Melanie often feel. If the vending machines were empty, "as a last resort," she would rifle through the communal kitchen on her hall, taking whatever she could find. Under such circumstances, the food might be quite unsavory: whole boxes of crackers, loaves of bread, even raw sugar. If she was lucky enough to come on something tasty like a yogurt or bag of cookies, the next day she would be in trouble with the classmate whose food she pilfered. When Melanie was able to go to a store and buy food for a binge, she could "treat" herself to things like cookies, cake, potato chips, dips, and candy. People characteristically binge on such high carbohydrate, junk food.

Another week, Melanie noted she often binged to reverse an absence of feelings, "just to feel something." At these times she felt "empty" and "numb." A binge, with its bloated feeling and even low back pain, served to jolt her out of this ennui.

Next, Melanie observed she binged after fleeing social situations in which she felt alienated or bored. This might be a classroom discussion in which she felt "out of it." Or she might be at a student party and begin to feel "disconnected" or "unpopular" and flee the scene, believing she was a "failure" for not being fully engaged with others. Here, in addition to assuaging alienation, binging was also a form of self-punishment.

Finally, Melanie observed an impulse to binge in any confrontational situation, whenever she felt angry or frustrated dealing with someone. This was the enraged underside of the eating disorder. In the prototypic scene, Melanie would be angry with another person but unable to express herself. Instead she would "take it" and "stuff it" emotionally. At the first opportunity, she would stuff herself with food. She then obtained some relief from vomiting up the food in an unconscious ritual, symbolic of her unexpressed emotions. In these instances, even more guilt and self-recrimination were entangled in the disturbed eating behavior, because Melanie felt so uncomfortable with her anger.

This was a sophisticated stage in the therapy, elucidating the many facets of Melanie's behavior. Particularly when her eating disorder expressed contortions around frustration and anger, Melanie could see the relationship with her mother writ large.

She said, "I had to keep so much in, I had to stifle so much, in order to conform to her wishes. . . . I vomited all over her expectations to be thin, normal, and successful. I punished myself for not being happy to live up to those standards while at the same time punishing her. She never liked it. She hated the vomiting."

"How did she know about your vomiting?"

"She's very aware when it comes to food. When she saw me eating a lot and not gaining weight, she suspected. At times, I left more obvious clues."

"Such as?"

"If I didn't clean up the bathroom completely she'd find lingering smells or traces of vomit and be disgusted."

"So many children do this in one form or another," I reflected aloud to Melanie. "They feel so guilty about being angry at parents, that they do something self-destructive as a way of hurting the parents indirectly. In the process, they hurt themselves even more, but that makes it palatable. Even as they punish the parents, they protect them from the full force of their fury."

I pointed out to Melanie that a binge also expressed her yearnings, her desire to fill her emptiness, to be nourished and comforted by food (What better symbol of mothering?), but at the same time, the vomiting expressed her angry rejection of the nurturing she felt to be so woefully inadequate. Her eating disorder embodied a remarkable combination of both her yearnings and hostile rejection.

This type of frustrating, enmeshed mother-daughter relationship is the most common core of an eating disorder. Not that the father is insignificant. Sometimes he is an idealized figure whom the daughter would like to emulate as an alternative to the mother but he is too distant, remote, and unavailable for this purpose. Or, as in Melanie's case, the father is not a mitigating influence because he is weak. But nearly always, the mother-daughter relationship is central.

From this vantage point, one can see the symptomatology of an eating disorder as a failed attempt to achieve a stronger sense of self. It is a repeated effort to assert oneself, to take in what one needs and, at the same time, to reject or protest. The disturbed eating behavior is a distorted expression of these deep sentiments. On the one hand, it is doomed to fail but, on the other hand, it represents the individual's effort to keep hope alive. The object of therapy is to make all this clear to the patient and encourage her to reinvest the energy in more productive ways.

For someone with an eating disorder, food is no longer an inanimate object; feeding is not merely a physiological function. Instead, it is heavily invested with conflictual psychological meaning. Interestingly, one only sees this kind of distortion of eating behavior in luxury societies where food is in abundance. Only under such circumstances do people overeat and vomit, even starve themselves to death, out of psychological anger and hunger. One does not see eating disorders in underdeveloped countries where, in short supply, food is still yoked to biological necessity and not available to assume such distorted, symbolic meaning.

Our discussions began to demystify food and the ritual of eating for Melanie. Several months into therapy, life was more manageable for her and there was no more talk of dropping out of school. Melanie went home for just a few days over the Christmas break because she had so much work to do preparing for exams in January. True to form, she did well on the exams and got high grades. This reassured her she would do well in college, allaying fears she was a "mistake" on the part of the Harvard admissions committee.

Early in the second semester, Melanie began a relationship with a young man, another undergraduate. Like her earlier boyfriends, he was on the domineering side. This provided new opportunities for Melanie to assert herself and work on healthier relationships. Her bulimia continued to decrease.

Then, at spring break, Melanie went home to her parents in Chicago for ten days. To her dismay, her eating disorder reappeared forcefully. "Whereas I had been binging less than once a week, suddenly I was back to doing it every day, sometimes more than once a day."

"What do you think happened?" I asked.

"I don't know," Melanie said, quite upset. "I felt like I just walked in the door and couldn't help myself."

On reflection, Melanie realized her bulimia had taken a

few days to gather force. Still, to her there was something irresistible and mysterious about what happened. In response to my questions about what upset her, Melanie could only say she found aspects of her relationship with her mother "disturbing."

One often sees this pattern in people recovering from self-destructive behavior with roots in family dynamics: When the behavior is markedly decreased and under considerable control, it may flare up during visits home. This is because of the strong regressive pull, falling into old patterns of behavior and ways of relating to parents. In a variation on this theme, the behavior may remain in control during the visit but flare up right after leaving, while traveling, or immediately upon return. The association is striking and often startling to patients. If the patient had any doubts before, this phenomenon irrefutably establishes a link between the behavior and the nexus of family ties.

In the weeks following her visit home, Melanie tried to sidestep the psychological issues and work more pragmatically on bringing her eating under control again. She had partially succeeded when, about two weeks after returning from her trip, she came to a session distraught because she had a "major binge."

"That hasn't happened at school for months," said Melanie tearfully. "I feel like I'm permanently set back. Will I ever overcome this?"

"I doubt this is permanent," I responded. "Progress always comes in waves: You take two steps forward and one step back. This is definitely a setback but, hopefully, a productive one, especially if we can figure out what happened during your visit home."

Melanie said the binge two days before had been precipitated by an argument with her boyfriend. They were at a party together when Melanie began to feel alienated and bored. She told her boyfriend she wanted to leave, but he declined. When she pressed, her boyfriend was rude, leaving Melanie feeling "stung." Shortly after their argument, a "switch flipped" in her head, and Melanie decided she would binge. This brought some immediate relief, allowing her to remain at the party a while longer. Finally, she left without her boyfriend. On her way home, she stopped at a convenience store and bought two bags of junk food. Arriving home, she locked herself into her room and "did it."

Melanie and I had never discussed a binge in detail. At some point in therapy this is important to do. A detailed description of the behavior inevitably sheds new light on it. In Melanie's case, it revealed a whole new dimension.

"What did you do?" I inquired.

At first, Melanie stared at me as if to say, "You really want to know?" I stared back until she began her story. Once inside her room, Melanie took off her coat and put it away. She kicked her shoes into the closet, too. Going over to her stereo, she put on a tape of Bruce Springsteen, which she described as "low, sensual, rhythmic music." Then, preparing to binge, she undressed quickly.

"Do you always undress?" I asked, surprised.

"If I'm in my room, yes," Melanie said, slightly embarrassed. "I'm happiest to eat in bed, in a favorite old satin nightgown."

Melanie put the bags of food on the floor beside the bed, so she could "just reach over" each time she wanted more. She described a "perverse pleasure" in unwrapping food, opening it, and reaching inside. As she gorged and listened to the rhythm of the music, she fell into a "kind of trance."

"Another thing I do . . . ," Melanie started to say, self-consciously. "I ran a hand under my nightgown and began caressing myself. I gently massaged my breasts, abdomen, and thighs."

Melanie fed until her abdomen was completely full, until she felt bloated, her senses pleasantly dulled. This was a severe, or major, binge meaning she pushed herself to eat until the point of low back pain. Finally, when she could eat no more, Melanie got up.

"You see, I can't wait too long because I don't want to digest any of the food."

Going to her closet, Melanie picked out a clean set of clothes and laid them on the bed. Then she crossed the hall to the bathroom.

"I don't have to use a finger any more to induce vomiting. Now it's a reflex. As always, puking was climactic. I felt a huge sense of relief. Vomiting cleared my head; I slowly came to, emerging from the bloated, senseless feeling."

After vomiting, Melanie felt "energized again." She cleaned up after herself and took a shower. Back in her room she dressed in the clean set of clothes she had set out. Melanie described feeling a pleasant mixture of being "depleted and refreshed."

"I felt energized enough that I stayed up studying for an hour."

Reflecting on what she told me, Melanie concluded, "Not all binges are so perfect. It's different when you binge in a restaurant and have to use a bathroom stall. . . . Still, it has something of the same energy. When my boyfriend came by in the morning, I felt fine. All the anger and frustration with him had disappeared."

Melanie had described her binge in a mesmerizing way, capturing both its distasteful and, for her, appealing aspects. We discussed how the graphic details substantiated our earlier interpretation of her behavior: The need to allay anger and frustration. Food as a way of filling and comforting herself. Vomiting as an emotional discharge. But the detailed description also revealed something new, the strong sexual overtones: The aphrodisiac state. The semiconscious mixture of purposefulness and abandon. The palpable connection between eating and sexuality.

After discussing other aspects of the scene, I commented to Melanie on the sexual innuendo.

"Where?" Melanie frowned.

"Throughout," I responded. "Beginning with the rhythmic music and undressing. Caressing yourself while you gorge. Vomiting is climactic. Afterward you're a mixture of depleted and refreshed."

"I guess so . . . ," Melanie conceded unconvincingly.

"That never occurred to you?"

"No."

"I'm surprised. In fact, I wondered if you were implying you masturbated."

"No!" said Melanie.

"Do you ever masturbate?"

Melanie shook her head.

"Even apart from binges?"

"Never."

"Why not?"

"Masturbate? I'm not interested in that. It's . . . dirty."

Dirty, I thought to myself.

As though reading my mind, Melanie reflected, "Does that sound odd coming from someone who makes herself vomit?"

A connection between eating disorders and sexuality should not be altogether surprising. For eating-disordered women, the body has become the battleground for their psychological conflicts. Eating involves oral, and therefore potentially sexual, drives. But for Melanie, the sexual part had been split off and unconscious.

In subsequent sessions, when Melanie and I returned to the subject of sexuality, in addition to *dirty,* she used words like *bad* and *selfish* to describe masturbation. Never comfortable discussing sexuality, her parents "acknowledged" intercourse in the context of discouraging it. She "could not imagine" either of her parents "breathing" the word *masturbate.* It was even more embarrassing and shameful than intercourse.

When I asked if she ever experimented with overt self-stimulation, Melanie said no. She had a vague recollection of being severely reprimanded as a child for playing with herself. This cast a pall on sexuality and is not uncommon in the lives of women. Melanie was embarrassed to admit she did not even know herself "down there." Earlier Melanie said her boyfriends decided when they slept together. Now she described in more detail her passive role in sexual relationships, which failed to allow her to integrate genital sexuality even as she participated in intercourse.

I thought Melanie's passive, dissociated relationship to sexuality mirrored the rest of her life. This was another example of her lack of connection with herself, her feelings, even her own body. Her experience, conflicts, and attitudes are not uncommon. Whereas nearly all men masturbate, many women do not. Women's sexual anatomy is less visible and more complicated than men's. Even well-educated women can be woefully ignorant of and estranged from their sexuality.

This is an area that has been well addressed by the

women's movement. In the last two decades a number of good illustrated books have appeared that teach female anatomy and the practical aspects of masturbating. Other books are available to help women develop sexual fantasy lives.

After discussing her sexual conflicts, I encouraged Melanie to get to know herself better sexually. I recommended a book for the purpose and the use of a small, hand-held mirror to facilitate self-exploration. It took Melanie some time to "get up the courage" to buy the book and begin experimenting.

Eventually Melanie reported back that she was masturbating regularly. She most liked to masturbate in front of a full-length mirror in a new self-pleasuring ritual that helped supplant her more self-destructive eating ritual. I liked the idea of Melanie admiring her body in the mirror, because body image and self-esteem are important issues for women with eating disorders. Melanie's growing sexual self-awareness also influenced her relationship with her boyfriend. She began expressing herself more freely with him, making known her sexual needs.

Melanie's sexual awakening was a proportionately small yet important part of her treatment, a landmark in her growing self-possession and mastery. When we returned to the subject of her visit home, she was able to be more articulate about what disturbed her. Melanie realized food was "just about the only thing" she and her mother could discuss. More clearly than ever, she saw her mother as preoccupied with dieting, looking well, shopping, buying clothes, and comparing herself with others.

"I got so depressed," said Melanie, "going around to malls with her."

When Melanie brought up a subject she was interested

in—an English class, a book, or some other intellectual pursuit—her mother would dismiss her, saying, "Oh, the grand ideas you're learning at that college of yours."

"She makes me feel so guilty," said Melanie, "that I shut up. I stop bringing my ideas into our conversations."

"Which is to say you stop being yourself."

"Exactly. I think she feels threatened. What I really think is she's not interested. She lives almost exclusively in a world of material things. We don't have many interests in common but she wouldn't want to admit it. So she gets defensive. It's sad to think all the education and advantages she wanted for me have estranged us."

"It is very sad," I replied.

While she was at her parents' house, Melanie observed she sometimes acquiesced to discussing food, dieting, and weight with her mother "so we had something to talk about."

"She has endless energy for critiquing me . . . whether I've lost or gained weight, what I wear, how I look. When I was really cynical during the trip, I thought it was because food and diet are the one area where she can win. I can never be as thin as she is, as thin as she would like me to be."

Melanie observed that her mother gave mixed messages and played food games with her. She remembered, "One night we went to a restaurant for dinner. She had a huge dessert and more or less challenged me to do the same. Only hours before, she'd told me I needed to lose weight."

These were painful realizations for Melanie.

"I hate to think she's jealous," Melanie said tearfully, "of the same accomplishments she encouraged me in and was so proud of."

Melanie and I discussed the larger social, as well as personal, issues here. That is, the often unfortunate gap between mothers and daughters in her generation. All too often nowadays, mothers and daughters look at one another across a wide gulf of different expectations and opportunities available to women in their respective generations.

Through these discussions, Melanie developed a more sympathetic view of her mother, with her failed ambitions and financial dependence on her husband. Such a sympathetic view is often a relief to patients. However, it is only possible at this stage in therapy. Earlier on it would be antagonistic with the necessary task of getting in touch with the anger and disappointment.

In the realm of larger social issues, Melanie and I also discussed our culture's preoccupation with thinness in women, which echoed her mother's demands. Thinness bordering on the unhealthy is widely touted in our pervasive media. For eating-disordered women, this cultural icon is often a dangerous lure. Few people can meet the advertised ideal but the market forces in our society seem intent on making the majority of people feel badly about themselves, perhaps as a way of driving cosmetic, apparel, and athletic consumption.

Eventually, Melanie acknowledged she had a body that, while not ultrathin, was trim and healthy-looking. As she grew in self-possession and her own set of values, she became more self-accepting, relaxed, and even proud of her body.

Few people make the connection between eating and sexuality as vividly as Melanie had, but to varying degrees it is often present. The old psychoanalytic literature emphasized a sexual interpretation of eating disorders. Unfortunately, this was often done to excess, ignoring other important psychosocial factors, such as those elucidated early on with Melanie. However, many modern, antiseptic approaches have abandoned the old ideas completely, losing important clinical pearls in the process.

Eating disorders usually appear in puberty, coincident with the disorienting changes in a woman's body: the hormonal changes, onset of menses, redistribution of fat, and development of breasts and other curves of the mature female figure. The most extreme of eating-disordered women, anorexics, arrest their maturational and sexual growth. Their periods cease, the curves in their bodies stop developing, and they retain the boyish figures of their childhood. While not frankly anorexic, many other women suppress their menses with precipitous dieting or compulsive exercise. At the opposite end of the spectrum, some women say they make themselves overweight fearing admiration and sexual advances from men.

Connections between food and sexuality are hardly limited to eating disorders. Many women say explicitly they eat more when not in a sexual relationship. Historical, literary, and mythological associations between food and sex abound. Roman vomitoria were the sites of all kinds of licentiousness. The mischievous god Bacchus reveled in gastronomic and sexual excess.

Most men have difficulty comprehending the relationship women have to food. However, lest one fall into the current separatist trap, one need not look far for an analogy in the world of men. In our culture, exercise and body building are to men what dieting and being thin are to women. These are the two body-image obsessions fostered in our media. Extremes of exercising in men can be as ambitious and self-punishing as extremes of dieting in women.

In the previous chapter, "Don Juan's Regret," Rick is a typical example of the male wrapped up in his self-image. In psychotherapy one sees a curious parallel between the sexes.

As they begin to feel better, often men report starting to exercise again. As in Rick's case, coming to a psychotherapy session with an exercise bag in hand is a telltale sign the patient's mood has improved. At the same psychological juncture, many women will announce starting a diet. Men say that exercising is good for their self-esteem in exactly the same way that women say dieting is.

Whereas Melanie felt she could discuss only food with her mother, Rick felt he could discuss only sports with his father. In both instances, issues of body image and self-esteem ultimately went back to a poor relationship with the same-sex parent, not adequately mitigated by the relationship with the opposite-sex parent.

Noxious Balms:
The Mysterious Sexual
Inhibitor and
the Disappearing Sperm

Sometimes sexual problems and their solutions are a small piece of a larger psychotherapy. While it may be a discrete problem, the sexual concern can play a decisive role at a critical point in the therapy. The patient's bringing the problem up may result from a new level of distress with the difficulty. It may also signal a new level of trust in the therapist. Helping the patient solve the sexual problem may go a long way, at a crucial juncture in the therapy, toward strengthening the therapeutic alliance between patient and doctor. This was true in the two cases described below: John, who was somewhat skeptical and reserved entering psychotherapy, and Chris, a schizophrenic young man who was tentative in all his engagements.

John described himself as a "modern man" trying, as yet unsuccessfully, to juggle work and family life. He had a demanding job and young family, a wife and two sons. He felt he was burning the candle at both ends, becoming exhausted and confused. Unable to effect change on his own, he sought professional help to "sort out his priorities and map a course of change."

In his mid-thirties when he consulted me, John described himself as a "1960s child" with a pressurized career he never expected to have. As a youth he dropped out of college to tour with a rock band. Although they never made "celebrity status," John and the other members of the band had a wonderful time for five years, performing and traveling in this country and abroad.

At the end of five years, a little burned out and exhausted, the group broke up, its members dispersing to finish their educations and take up more conventional careers. John went back to college to finish the last year of his bachelor's degree. During that year he met the woman who would be his wife. After graduating, they traveled together, taking up residence and jobs for varying periods of time on the East and West coasts. Only at age thirty did John become serious about a job for the first time. Two factors conspired to bring this change about: His wife was pregnant with their first child, and he joined a small entrepreneurial company headed by a charismatic man fifteen years his senior.

"I've been at the job seven years now," said John with a mixture of chagrin and pride. "That's the longest I've done anything, and my life has metamorphosed in those years."

The company specialized in optical lenses, supplying manufacturers of everything from microscopes to cameras.

"The only other thing I was good at besides music," John said, "was mathematics. I knew nothing about lenses and optics but I was able to learn the technical and manufacturing side of things quickly. I took instantly to the entrepreneurial environment. It had some of the excitement I thought I'd left behind with my madcap days of performing. The owner of the company and I hit it off, and I gradually became his right-hand man. He is always in the clouds with his ideas and needed someone reliable to follow through for him. I've been somewhat reluctantly swept along into this snowballing career."

The last year had been particularly difficult. John had to travel more than usual on business. He hated being away from his family. Being away meant his work piled up, creating more to do when he was in town. His hours on the job were "ever expanding." He made a point of never working Saturday afternoons or Sundays, and on week nights he tried to be home by seven or eight but often was not.

"My twenties and the first few years I had kids—in my early thirties—weren't like this at all. My career wasn't a high priority. Music, having a good time, my marriage, and finally my children were the high priorities. Now I have a more serious career and I feel an obligation to provide well for my kids. But I'm torn because I feel I'm missing too much of their childhoods. They will never be this age again. My son is playing baseball now and I hardly ever get to go to his games. That hurts."

John briefly looked as though he might get emotional talking about his relationship with his son but moved away from this quickly. On a more intellectual level he continued, "I read a lot about the difficulty modern women have juggling careers and family life but I think it's hard for modern men too. Every man I know is struggling with it. Our fathers seem to fall into two camps: those who were emotionally uninvolved with the family, off pursuing demanding careers, providing well materially but emotionally not there, versus those who were present in the home all the time but whose careers went nowhere. Neither is much of a model for how to lead a balanced life."

In addition to competing with his children, the job was also a strain on John's marriage. His wife, Peggy, thought his career was "out of control."

"One of the things that's been a problem in the past five years," said John, "is the very different paths my wife and I have taken. We used to do everything together. We both worked or we were traveling together. Since the children, particularly the second, she's really been focused on child rearing and I've believed it is my job to provide. I don't feel she quite understands the conflict for me of wanting to spend more time with the family versus every time it comes up that they need one more thing—a new outfit now, braces or college in the future—I think I need to work harder to provide."

"How does Peggy respond when you say that?" I asked. Her point of view would provide a different angle on the situation.

"She says there's an element of truth to it but the real problem is I don't set limits well enough at work. On the one hand I don't delegate enough and on the other I can't say no to my boss. As a result, my work is endless."

"Is she right?"

John did not like admitting it but said, "There's some truth to it."

His wife had strongly encouraged John to enter therapy. A close male friend who recently started therapy encouraged him to as well. About three weeks before he first saw me, John went to his internist concerned about his overwork, exhaustion, stress, and a possible ulcer.

"I don't have an ulcer. All the tests were negative. But I'm on antacids. I figure next it will be blood pressure pills.

My internist suggested I see you before I reach that point."

Some time before, John had planned a three-week family vacation which was now only two months away.

"I thought that might be the change I needed. We haven't had a proper vacation in years. While I was planning it and for a short while afterward, I felt much better. Then that began to erode and I realized a vacation wasn't going to be enough. I figured enough people had recommended therapy, I should try it even though I'm skeptical."

In the first two months we worked together, before John's family vacation, I found him thoughtful, sensitive, and intelligent. The breadth of his interests, the rock-musician-turned-executive, suggested a range of talents and flexibility, which was intriguing. His dilemma of juggling work and family life was certainly poignant and widespread among contemporary men.

Outwardly, John was quite engaged in therapy. He was dutiful about his appointments, always on time, in spite of his busy schedule. However, I thought he was holding back. He was inclined to keep our discourse at a pragmatic level: how to limit his hours at work versus providing adequately for his children. He steered away from emotionally charged topics such as how his relationship with his wife had changed in recent years or his relationships with his sons. With his rational, mathematical mind he spoke of wanting to "chart a course for change" clearly hoping this would be a simple, linear task. I sensed he was being cautious about how much he opened up. This is quite common among men when they first enter psychotherapy. Men are not socialized to acknowledge their vulnerabilities readily or ask for help. I was patient, knowing that over time this would likely change.

Recalling John's comment that men of his father's generation fell into two categories, I asked one day which kind of father he had. With what I thought was a touch of embarrassment he said, "My father was the type who was home a lot but whose career went nowhere."

As we talked further it emerged that John's mother was never satisfied materially with what the father was able to provide. As a result, John felt "conscripted" into being an ambitious son. He spent years flouting his parents', particularly his mother's, ambitions for him, dropping out of college to be a musician, which to them was being a "bum."

"But even then," said John, "there was a certain amount of ambition, the slim chance I'd have made it big. I didn't just sit on a curb and smoke dope for five years."

When the music "trip" ran aground, John "reentered the fold" reluctantly. Only when he stumbled into an exciting job, at the same time as he became a father and felt the need to provide more security for his family, did his drive and ambition become manifest in a forceful way.

Just before he left for vacation, John suggested his current dilemma with his career was something of an all-or-nothing phenomenon: Because he had flouted the mantle of ambition for so many years, once he "bought into the system"—with a family, job, and boss he liked—it was hard for him to keep a check on his ambition.

I suspected John's all-or-nothing approach was the reason why he had trouble setting limits at work, more so than his concerns to provide well for his children. Was he struggling with his internalization of his parents' ambitions for him, whether resisting them or being unable to keep them in check? Did he need above all to be different from his father, either outside the system, pretending not to care, or inside, working himself too hard to be sure he succeeded? Was he fearful that spending more time at home would cause his career to collapse, like his father's? Was his charismatic boss a father figure, the type of father he never had and one to whom he could not say no? This vague but potentially fruitful realm was just coming over the horizon when John went with his family on their three-week vacation.

John returned from vacation tanned and looking refreshed. The vacation was "wonderful" for him and his family. He spoke of "never having relaxed so much with his children." At the same time, he was agitated. He felt "like he hadn't been away long enough." The transition back to work was proving difficult because he was "under so much stress."

For most of the session John was all over the place, contradicting himself, seeming rejuvenated and at the same time exasperated. He did not make sense until near the end of the meeting when he blurted out that he had been having a sexual problem with his wife, which disappeared while they were on vacation, only to return once they were back.

Clearly flustered and embarrassed, John labeled the problem "impotence." He had not mentioned it before, hoping it would go away of it's own accord. Indeed, it emerged he had hoped therapy would lift his spirits sufficiently that this problem would fade without his having to deal with it directly.

"Was this a large part of why you came into therapy?"

"Yes and no," John equivocated. "I suppose it's just one more symptom. Peggy had been urging me to tell you."

It occurred to me that this problem and John's reticence about it probably accounted for his reserve, my feeling that he was holding back, in the first two months of our work. John said he went on vacation never expecting the problem to improve in such a short span of time. He was "dismayed" when he and his wife tried intercourse in the second week of the vacation and "everything went fine." He was even more shocked when the problem returned once he was back to work.

"I guess this means it's definitely the stress of my job," John said in desperation. "What am I going to do? I can't change that too quickly. From now on am I always going to be impotent when I'm under pressure?"

I cautioned John against jumping to conclusions. There were many possible causes of his sexual dysfunction, which we would need to explore. As we were at the end of the meeting, we agreed to discuss the possibilities in detail the next week.

In the following session, John commented on how difficult it had been to tell me about his sexual problem. "I've never told anyone before, especially a man, that I was having trouble doing something central to my identity as a man. I thought back to when I played sports and was having trouble mastering something new. I never admitted it to anyone. I always toiled away stoically."

John and I began to review the list of questions germane to sexual function: medical history, family and religious background, attitudes toward sexuality, sexual history, and his relationship with his wife.

John said he had been impotent for the past ten months. When I asked him to clarify what he meant, he said, "I can't get it up. I'm not interested in sex. It's like my whole energy for sex has flattened. Before the vacation, Peggy and I hadn't had intercourse in nearly a year."

As we talked I thought John's problem sounded more like diminished interest in sex (a decreased libido) rather than impotence (the inability to maintain an erection to effect intercourse). John noted that the time frame of the problem corresponded roughly with the stressful year he had had, further evidence to him that work-related anxiety was the cause.

John had never had sexual difficulties before in his life, even when under considerable pressure. Before the past year, his sexual relationship with his wife had been excellent. As his problem developed, she was sympathetic and understanding. More recently, she urged him to get help.

"Has she become impatient or demanding?" I asked. While the circumstances might make such a response understandable, if a spouse takes this position it always makes matters worse.

John said no, Peggy had not become in any way reproachful. In the second half of the year, he began using methods other than intercourse to bring her to orgasm for her sexual relief. What he had not told Peggy was that even this was fairly mechanical and not arousing to him. John said he thought their sex life was a "half measure"; he felt "compromised." He was glad Peggy was not happy with the status quo. She obviously cared about their relationship.

"Could the problem be encroaching middle age?" John speculated aloud. "I'm almost forty."

This proved to be a serious concern of John's. Before the development of his sexual problem, for some time he noticed he was "slowing down" sexually. He took a little longer to be aroused and achieve an erection. Likewise, he was slower to orgasm.

"In general," said John, "I welcomed the changes in my sexual function. I felt more productive in life, less at the mercy of raging hormones. But impotence was more than I bargained for!"

I clarified again that I thought John's problem was not so much impotence as a decrease in his libido. At the same time, I reassured him his problem could by no means be the result of normal aging. He should not resign himself to the status quo.

"When the problem went away on vacation I, too, realized it couldn't be age," he responded.

Continuing my inquiries, I asked John if he had ever been conflicted or inhibited sexually. He denied having any conflicts with "the possible exception of being fairly normal." When I asked what he meant by that, John said he was "not big on experimenting sexually." He was "happy most of the time with the missionary position" and "not into any kinky stuff." This was fairly conservative for a former rock musician.

John drank socially and for years had not used any other recreational drugs. We reviewed the quantity of his alcohol intake, which was indeed modest.

"Are you on any medications?" I inquired.

"No," said John.

Recalling one of our early meetings, I asked, "What about your stomach? I thought you were on antacids?"

"Oh, I didn't think to mention that. It's over-the-counter; just Maalox. I thought you meant serious drugs."

"No. I meant anything. Over-the-counter or otherwise."

"Well, antacids. Tylenol sometimes. And Valium."

"Valium?"

"Yes."

"Does your internist prescribe it?"

"No. It's my wife's. She's taken it on and off for years."

"How long have you been on it?"

"About a year," said John. Then he did a double take, realizing this was roughly the same time frame as his sexual difficulty.

"Did you take it on vacation?"

"No," said John dismayed. "I forgot to pack it and didn't need it I was so relaxed."

"And you've gone back on it since you came home?"

"Yes. I've been stressed out again. You're not suggesting the Valium could have anything to do with my problem, are you? It's pretty benign."

I explained to John that Valium was relatively benign but all medications have side effects. Most medications create new problems as they treat old ones. In some individuals, medications like Valium can cause a decrease in sex drive. John, as most people would be, was amazed. I also expressed my concern that medication would delay John's getting to the source of and resolving his anxieties.

We initiated a trial off the medication, tapering John from it. Sure enough his sexual problem disappeared again. Although surprised, John was relieved the cure was such a simple intervention. To palliate his fear of being without the medication I referred him to a biofeedback group to learn relaxation techniques.

Divulging his sexual problem and our being able to solve it went a long way toward eroding John's skepticism and reserve in psychotherapy, solidifying our alliance.

"If I could tell you about that," said John, "I can tell you anything."

This began a new phase in our work. John remained in therapy for a year, sorting through his conflicts at work and arriving at a new balance. John's relationship with the man he worked for did prove important. This man was a father figure. Being charismatic, he could also be quite demanding. Only after John could see the connection between his relationship with his parents and his boss could he begin to set limits with him. Slowly, he began to decline those requests from his boss that John thought went beyond a reasonable expectation for his job. In time, his boss accommodated and became less demanding. John began to delegate more work and, while maintaining the same standards, took himself and work a little less seriously. His case was an excellent example where resolving a sexual problem that emerged early on established a therapeutic alliance and moved the overall therapy forward. It is also an example of people's naïveté, in twentieth-century American culture, regarding medications and their benefits, risks, and side effects.

Another medication-related sexual problem involved less commonly used antipsychotics. Chris was a schizophrenic young man who was slightly disheveled and remote. He spoke with a paucity of words and a minimum of affect. Indeed, his whole life was minimal. He told me about his bare apartment and simple schedule, living on disability income.

Chris was looking for someone to do psychotherapy with him. Psychotherapy with schizophrenics is a dying art in an age of medical management and powerful pharmacologic agents. Chris found most clinicians "afraid" of his history of psychosis and "too quick to reach for pills" if he reported the slightest distress.

Chris had been an unusually intelligent youth with great promise when he had his first psychotic break early in college. His loneliness at being away from home and the pressure of a university environment precipitated his psychosis. He was hospitalized briefly and returned to his parents' home. In his late teens and early twenties, Chris gradually lowered his expectations for himself and his life-style. After becoming stable at this altered baseline, he returned to Boston where he had been living for several years.

Chris wanted to see if he could establish a rapport with a therapist and using that as a base, possibly return to school. He never finished his bachelor's degree, an enduring source of disappointment. He was interested in the degree for its own sake, not as an entrée into a career. He had adapted to a solitary life, was living on disability, and was not interested in working.

I encouraged Chris to return to school if and when he felt ready. He later told me this surprised and appealed to him, because earlier care givers told him never to attempt such a thing. To do so, they said, would be to set himself up for repeated failure.

Psychosis-prone individuals are easily overwhelmed by emotion. One thus proceeds slowly with someone like Chris. We began meeting for only half an hour, every other week, which is often all such isolated individuals can tolerate. Whereas with high-functioning, neurotic patients the therapist needs to be confrontational and directive at times, one avoids any hint of direction with psychosis-prone people, because they interpret it as intrusive. Gradually we increased the frequency and length of our appointments as Chris became more comfortable. About six months into our work, once Chris was more relaxed with me, one day he sheepishly reported a long-standing problem.

"When I masturbate, no sperm comes out. I get erections without a problem. When I orgasm I feel a normal physical rush but my sperm seems to have disappeared. I don't understand how everything can apparently be working fine except there's no sperm."

Chris had not mentioned his sexual concern to earlier clinicians because he was too embarrassed. Lightening up a bit on the subject, he said, "At first I thought it might be my psychosis: Either I was hallucinating I had an orgasm or I was hallucinating there was no sperm. But it's real and has worried me."

The culprit was Chris's medication. I explained that sometimes antipsychotic medications cause contraction of sphincters in various parts of the body. In the side effect he was suffering from, contraction of a small sphincter at the base of the penis creates a detour, rerouting sperm coming up from the testes. Instead of exiting out the penis the sperm is redirected into the bladder. The physical rush Chris felt when he masturbated was indeed ejaculation but his sperm then disappeared into his bladder. The condition is called retrograde ejaculation and is a benign one. However, it is disconcerting to most men; it is ordinarily reversed by a reduction in medication.

Chris said he would like to have his normal functioning back. Clearly relieved by the explanation and continuing to lighten up discussing sexual matters, he said jokingly, "In some ways it makes the job cleaner. I suppose I shouldn't complain. But it's very odd. I think normal functioning would be worth having to clean up after myself."

The only difficult part of treating this side effect is to balance reducing the medication with maintaining it at a level sufficient to keep the patient stable. Three modest reductions in Chris's medication, spaced gradually over time, eradicated the problem without change in Chris's clinical status. As is often the case, at a later date we were able to make more substantial reductions in Chris's medication once psychotherapy was well established as a support for him.

Chris cautiously returned to school after a year in therapy. He took just one course the first semester, which was a difficult transition. Thereafter, he took two courses a semester and after several years managed to finish his bachelor's degree. This was enormously gratifying to him, healing the wound of not finishing the degree earlier because of his original psychotic break.

As a result of his therapy and school, Chris found he liked being somewhat involved in the outside world. Gradually, he made friends and extended his social network. Instead of retreating to his isolated world, after graduation he took a part-time position in a bookstore that had a relaxed, low-key atmosphere.

The psychiatric profession is now recognizing the limitations of the symptomatic relief obtained with antipsychotic medications and the value of psychotherapy in helping schizophrenic and other psychosis-prone individuals regain human connection and meaning in their lives.

In general, ours is an overmedicated culture. Many commonly used medications can have profound noxious effects on sexual function: antianxiety agents, blood pressure pills, cardiac medications, antidepressants, and some painkillers to name just a few. Whenever a patient reports sexual problems, medication side effects are one of the first things a therapist attempts to rule out.

ANCIENT RITES: A REVERSAL

Some patients are vague or inaccurate in describing their problems. This is especially true in the sexual realm where taboo, privacy, and popular misconceptions often leave people with a combination of embarrassment and a limited vocabulary for articulating their difficulties. This was true of Carl and Lee, a Korean-American couple who consulted with me. In our initial evaluation meeting we had to go over their problem a number of times, in increasing detail, before a clear picture of their difficulties emerged.

Carl and Lee were a soft-spoken, appealing couple in their mid-twenties. They came from the same tightly knit Korean-American community, which they described as politically and socially very conservative. Carl was born in this country. Lee and her parents moved to the United States when she was ten, so her family was "even more steeped in the Old World culture, even more conservative."

They began seeing one another in high school. They clarified that this did not exactly mean dating. In their community dating in any serious way was discouraged at the high school level. Adolescents were expected to devote most all of their time to studying and academic achievement. A boy or girl might have one, perhaps two, extracurricular interests such as playing a musical instrument or participating in a sport.

The tradition of adolescence being a time when one concentrated almost exclusively on one's studies in preparation for one's career and future had its roots in Korea. For nearly a century, Korean secondary school students have sat for national exams at the end of high school. These exams are crucial, because one's scores determine job prospects and future educational opportunities. With so much pressure on studying and performing well on these exams, dating is seen as a potential distraction. Through high school, boys and girls attend single-gender schools and have only limited opportunities to meet members of the opposite sex. There is little dating, as it is known in the United States, until college. Korean-American culture is not quite so rigid, but the influence is still strong. There is a lot of pressure for academic achievement, and what dating goes on is largely platonic.

At the college level expectations change, and that is when Carl and Lee began dating. However, they were at different colleges so their relationship was a long-distance one. For graduate school, they arranged to be in the same city but were unable to live together because they were not married. Moreover, their families opposed marrying before their professional education was complete.

When they came to see me, the couple had been married six months. Carl was a lawyer and Lee a systems analyst. They were well educated and articulate, but their demeanor changed when they began discussing the specific problem for which they came to see me.

"We have a sexual problem," Carl began hesitantly.

"I see," I said, nodding.

Carl and Lee glanced uncomfortably at one another and

me for some moments. They seemed uncertain about how to proceed. Which one of them was going to speak first? Who would say what about their difficulties?

Eventually, Lee said awkwardly, "We haven't been able to . . . to consummate our marriage." Looking to Carl, she asked, "Do you want to tell the next part?"

Carl explained that sex was never discussed in their cultural milieu, even among close friends, making it extremely difficult for them to talk about their concern. He then blurted out the words *impotent* for himself and *frigid* for Lee. Having gotten that far in describing the problem, he asked anxiously, "What is the cure?"

"Well," I said gently, "I would need to know more about you—your history and what you mean by the words *impotent* and *frigid*—before I could suggest a treatment."

Crestfallen to think they would have to explain in any more detail, they asked, "What do you want to know?"

"How you got to this point sexually. What your relationship was like before marriage. And what the six months since your wedding have been like."

Slowly, they explained that their protracted courtship and engagement had produced considerable sexual tension between them. Unable to resist, they developed a fairly involved sexual relationship, "without having intercourse."

"We didn't want either of us to turn to other outlets," said Carl attempting to justify their sexual liaison. "We wanted to be monogamous and contain our sexuality within the relationship. Our religion is just as negative about masturbation as it is about premarital sex. So if we were going to have a sexual outlet, if we were going to break the rules, we figured we may as well do it with one another."

Carl tried to say the last sentence with humor but it fell flat. He was clearly uncomfortable with the history of their premarital sexual involvement. In his attempt to justify it, Carl was projecting on to me the harsh criticism he would expect from his background. Lee probably felt the same or worse, I thought.

Indeed, she broke in tearfully, "In our community we're something of a model couple. It's an ideal if you fall in love with someone right in your own backyard whom you've known all your life. Of course no one had any idea we had a sexual relationship. People would be shocked." Letting slip her worst fear, Lee said, "Maybe that's why we're having a problem now."

"You feel guilty?"

"Ashamed. I tried not to at the time. But with the trouble we've had, I can't help thinking maybe that's why."

"You're concerned your difficulty now is punishment for what you did earlier?"

"Yes."

Could they tell me more about their religious background, I asked. They explained that the Korean church has a pervasive influence on the national culture. It is a Protestant sect, quite narrow and rigid. Sex before marriage is "out of the question" for both men and women. Virginity at marriage is "totally assumed."

"The position is not just moralistic," said Lee. "For example, my mother told me in no uncertain terms I should be a virgin when I was married unless I was not married by the age of thirty, and then I should go ahead and have sex."

"Why did she say that?" I asked.

"She was trying to say it was something not to be missed in life but you should try to do it a certain way."

"I see. That's not something a Western European, Catholic, parent would say."

"That's what I mean by it's not just moralistic. There's

also this pragmatic element that ties in with what we were saying earlier about education. There is a prescribed order in which you are supposed to do things in life. Of course, it's very strongly held, and you feel ashamed to deviate from it."

"You keep using the word *shame* when I would use the word *guilt*," I commented.

"Yes," they said, smiling.

Carl explained, "Asians feel shame when Westerners would feel guilt. It's not so much one's struggle with an internalized moral code. Rather, it's more one's sense of duty and obligation to the family and community, and one's shame in letting them down."

Carl, in fact, did not feel as ashamed as Lee about their premarital sexual relationship.

"I'm not sure everyone would be 'shocked' we had a sexual relationship," he said to Lee. "I think that's too strong. Korean-American communities are a little more enlightened than that. I think your parents, who are relatively recent immigrants, would be shocked."

Lee agreed, but also countered, "It's easier for Carl to be less ashamed. He would be held less accountable."

"There's a double standard?" I asked.

"Not officially. But men are more easily forgiven for sexual transgressions," Lee answered.

While Carl saw no causal link between the couple's premarital sex and their current dilemma, he was "troubled and perplexed" by their problem. He implied that while not feeling too ashamed at present, he could fall prey to it if another explanation and treatment were not found.

Within a religious framework, I said, one could conceive of Carl and Lee's difficulty as punishment for earlier deeds. However, I was not working in such a framework. Obviously, they consulted me for alternative views and solutions.

I reassured them I in no way judged them negatively for whatever sexual activity they had engaged in.

I commented that whatever shame the couple did feel could be holding them back: feeling ashamed for partaking of forbidden pleasures before marriage, they might now feel undeserving of the ultimate pleasure, intercourse, within marriage. We would keep this possibility in mind while investigating other potential causes. I reassured them that in all likelihood their problem, whatever its cause, would be treatable.

Having visibly put Carl and Lee at some ease, I said I needed to know more about their sexual histories. I knew this was difficult for people who had never acknowledged their sex life to anyone before, let alone discussed it, but it was essential.

Somewhat hesitantly the couple told me the following history: Their sexual activity began while they were in college, when home on vacation or visiting one another at school. Once engaged and living in the same city they felt better about what they were doing and freer. During their long engagement they had sex three or four times a week. By then they had progressed from kissing to petting to masturbation, mutual masturbation, and finally oral sex.

In the premarital sex, both Carl and Lee had no difficulty being fully aroused and reaching orgasm. Indeed that was "the norm."

"Did you try intercourse?" I inquired.

"Just a few times," Carl answered, "but we never managed it."

"What happened?"

"Not what happens now. It wasn't this impossible situation. We would both be very aroused. We'd fumble around a little. I never actually entered Lee. That's what it came down to. But it was no big deal. It wasn't like we panicked or lost our excitement. We went on and finished things as we usually did. It happened a very few times, maybe three or four, and we were always comfortable ascribing it to our mixed feelings. We didn't think of it in terms of failure, like we do now."

"Were the attempts at intercourse, or the sexual activity in general, initiated more by one of you than the other?"

"You mean did Carl pressure me?" asked Lee.

"Or vice versa."

"No. Never. It was mutual. On different occasions it might be one or the other of us who started things. But the feelings were always reciprocated."

On their wedding night the couple attempted intercourse and failed. Having looked forward to it, they made a more concerted effort than in the past. They ascribed this early failure to Carl's drinking on their wedding day. However, in the following weeks and months their sexual relationship gradually deteriorated. For a while the two continued to be fully aroused sexually. But with repeated failure at intercourse a vicious circle developed wherein they became increasingly fixed on coitus. As a result, their foreplay and noncoital forms of mutually reaching orgasm fell away. The more focused they became on effecting intercourse, the more miserably they failed. By about four months into the marriage neither of them could achieve sexual arousal. The past two months they had become aversive, almost phobic, about sex.

"Now I can't even get an erection," said Carl. "I've totally shut down sexually."

"So have I," said Lee. "I tense up. I don't want any sexual advances."

The couple reiterated their diagnoses: Carl's "impotence" and Lee's "frigidity."

"Which happened first? When you say you failed at intercourse, what exactly happened?" I inquired.

Once again the couple looked at me with some dismay.

"More details?" I could hear the question behind their stares.

How detailed a sexual history one needs is always a delicate matter. On the one hand many patients are so uncomfortable discussing sexual material, they need to feel a complete comfort on the therapist's part discussing any and all details. On the other hand, the therapist does not need to know everything, only enough to have a clear idea of what the problem is. But we had not yet reached that point. It was not yet clear what the true nature of Carl and Lee's problem was. For this reason it was important to continue.

Inquiring into a final level of detail, I said, "You have used the terms *impotent* and *frigid* for your difficulties, but I'm still not sure what you mean by that. You say you 'failed' at intercourse but that could have happened in a number of ways. Was the problem that Carl entered you, Lee, but then couldn't reach orgasm and lost his erection? Was it that he entered and was uncomfortable—or were you uncomfortable—and you had to stop? Or something else?"

"He never entered," Lee replied.

"He never got inside you?"

"I don't think so."

"Because you would lose your erections before entering?" I turned to Carl.

"I didn't lose my erections at that point," Carl said.

Lee declared, "I was in too much pain."

"Too much pain?"

"Yes. It hurt when he tried to enter."

"Did he try too soon, before you were ready?"

"No. In the first month or two I was having no trouble being aroused and ready."

"I would try to enter her," said Carl, "pressing with my penis. But it would hurt her so much I'd have to withdraw."

"You would withdraw?"

"I never really was inside."

"I see."

"I tried to guide him, you know, because at first we thought maybe he wasn't doing it right," said Lee, now only mildly flustered. One could see her making an effort to describe the important details. "I took over attempting to insert him, and it didn't make any difference."

"Eventually," said Carl, "we thought maybe I wasn't using enough force. So a few times I tried quite forcefully, with Lee's consent."

"What happened?"

"It hurt too much," said Lee. "It didn't work. We had to stop."

"That's when our sexual relationship completely fell apart," Carl sighed. "Here I was not succeeding and hurting Lee in the process. I couldn't bear it. I stopped being able to get erections."

"I began to question whether or not we were ever going to succeed," said Lee with tears welling in her eyes. "That's when I became ashamed of what we'd done before."

I was moved but also relieved. The problem was now clear to me. I was about to say so when Carl interjected, "I feel badly no matter which way I turn. Maybe we shouldn't have done what we did before marriage but another part of me feels I should have gotten even more experience. Some of my friends had a double standard. They got a lot more practice with women before their wives and they haven't had this problem. Sometimes I feel incompetent; like I, as the man, should have known more what to do and things would have been all right."

"Before you jump to conclusions," I said, "let me tell you where I think things stand. As you describe it, what I'm hearing is the real problem is penetration. That's why it was so important to go into the details. As I now see it, your 'impotence' and 'frigidity' are both secondary to a problem with penetration."

"What's the significance of that?" asked Lee.

"Well, it's very different, for example, than if the original problem was Carl developing impotence and you withdrawing sexually in response. Or, if it had been the other way around."

"Why?"

I explained that a problem with penetration raised very different concerns than a primary problem of impotence or frigidity. Pain and difficulty with penetration can result from a number of possible causes. By far the two most common are vaginismus and an intact hymen. Vaginismus is spasm of the vaginal musculature such that the penis cannot enter. The hymen is a thin membrane, sometimes quite strong, which covers the opening of the vagina. Nowadays an intact hymen is fairly rare because of tampons, gynecologic exams, and manipulation of the genitals during sexual activity. But they occasionally exist.

To my surprise, Lee said she had never had a gynecologic exam.

"Why not?" I asked.

"I've never had anything much wrong with me and in my family we only go to doctors when something is really wrong. That's an idiosyncrasy originating with my mother."

Lee had also never used tampons, preferring pads. In

none of her sexual activity had she ever been penetrated vaginally. This information led me to conclude an intact hymen was the most likely reason why the couple had not been able to consummate their marriage. It had not been a problem before then because of their mixed feelings about effecting intercourse. Once married and motivated to have intercourse, this physical impediment led to pain, frustration, and guilt. The two eventually withdrew sexually, Carl becoming "impotent" and Lee, "frigid."

I explained to Lee that she would need to see a gynecologist for a pelvic exam. Either an intact hymen or vaginismus would be diagnosed this way. If, as I suspected, the problem was an intact hymen a simple surgical procedure, called a hymenectomy, would remove the membrane from the vaginal orifice. If the problem was vaginismus, this would be treatable with behavioral techniques.

I discussed with Lee how difficult it might be to have a pelvic exam for the first time. She said she did not feel phobic about it and hoped it would not be a problem. I referred her to a particularly sensitive, relaxed gynecologist. I suggested Carl go with her and be present at the exam so they both saw what the problem was. In the unlikely event that neither of these problems was present, we would proceed to other possibilities. The couple thanked me and went off to see the gynecologist with a follow-up appointment with me in a few weeks.

When they returned Carl and Lee were beaming. Their problem had in fact been an unusually strong, intact hymen. Lee had already had the minor surgical procedure to remove it. Their sex life was immediately facilitated. One of the reasons for seeing the couple in follow-up was that sometimes the woman's, or man's, sexual withdrawal, conditioned by the painful obstacle to intercourse, can persist even after the hymen is removed. Occasionally, the woman can have concurrent vaginismus, which was established during the fitful attempts at intercourse. Any sexual dysfunction remaining after the surgery requires separate treatment. Fortunately, this was not the case for Carl and Lee.

The two expressed their joy at being relieved of the sexual difficulty. They appeared to have an excellent relationship, which had in no way contributed to their problem. Their cultural background with its sexual taboos had been a confounding variable in the case. The problem had been entirely mechanical, with a secondary overlay of psychological conflict and additional sexual dysfunction.

Carl and Lee's dilemma was in many ways a reversal of the historical position of an intact hymen. For much of human history an intact hymen has been a prized possession, shrouded in ancient rites and rituals. In some cultures a potential bride's honor rested on the presence of this tenuous membrane. Ritual inspections before marriage were often the rule. For example, among the Yungar, a seminomadic tribe in Australia, a future bride was deflowered by two older women one week before her marriage. If her hymen was not intact, the girl could be severely punished, even killed. In some cultures, stone phalli, horns, or other instruments were used in ritual deflorations. In other cultures, the couple's blood-stained bed sheets were paraded on their wedding night as proof of the bride's virginity. These are not just ancient rituals: As recently as the 1980s, Buckingham Palace announced on the eve of Charles's wedding that Lady Diana's virginity had been confirmed on physical examination by a palace physician. Royal rituals not withstanding, in most instances nowadays an intact hymen is a rare entity and a nuisance.

One final point regarding Carl and Lee: In my experience, the position of many Asian immigrant groups in the United States today is highly reminiscent of some Western European immigrants a few generations ago. One sees the clash of the old versus the new culture, particularly the wide gap between the first and second generations in this country. In the children, one sees the confusion and conflicts on issues like premarital sex, sexual identity, or deviation in any way from the parental norms. These are difficult transitions for both children and parents and often take several generations to resolve.

WHO WOULD HAVE EVER THOUGHT IT WOULD BE DIFFICULT TO GET PREGNANT?

R ecent generations have had unprecedented control over preventing pregnancy. Oral contraception—the Pill—was first introduced in the early 1960s. In addition to being far more effective than the previously popular condom or diaphragm methods, the Pill did not require any mechanical interruption of sexual activity. As a result, the Pill allowed couples more sexual freedom and spontaneity than ever before, virtually free from the anxiety of unwanted pregnancy.

More effective contraception also made it possible for people to postpone childbearing in the pursuit of careers and other interests. Since the Pill's introduction, dramatic social shifts have occurred. Couples now routinely delay having children until their thirties and even forties. Many people specifically aim to have two children in about a five-year period in their thirties. Unfortunately, nature cannot always be accommodating.

Indeed, many couples are unaware they are working against biology. For women, peak fertility occurs in the mid-twenties. In the thirties fertility declines, especially after age thirty-five.

Among men, normal sperm counts have dropped significantly in recent decades. According to some studies, the average sperm count is approaching half of what it was in the 1950s. While most men with these lower counts are still fertile, the trend is alarming. As yet, the cause is unknown. Speculation has centered on environmental toxins.

Unwittingly, the same generations who were the first to benefit from improved contraceptive technology now find themselves faced with increasing infertility. In the early 1980s, just twenty years after the Pill was introduced, the number of people seeking medical evaluation and treatment for infertility increased dramatically. Infertility is defined as a failure to conceive after one year of regular, unprotected intercourse. Estimates are that about 15 percent of couples, roughly one in seven, will have some degree of difficulty getting pregnant.

The growing numbers and resulting demand have fueled extraordinary growth in artificial, medical means of attempting pregnancy. We now possess a brave new world of reproductive high technology. Current procedures allow harvesting a woman's eggs, fertilizing them with sperm in a test tube, and transferring the resulting embryos back into the woman's uterus. If the man's sperm and/or woman's eggs are known to be defective, any combination of anonymous donor sperm and eggs may be substituted. If for some reason the woman cannot carry a pregnancy, the test tube embryo can be implanted in a surrogate mother to carry the couple's fetus to term.

Interestingly, these technological advances originated in

animal husbandry where they have been in use for almost a hundred years. For example, livestock breeders were traditionally limited in the number of offspring a prize female could produce in a lifetime. By contrast, prize males could sire unlimited progeny. Breeders now routinely circumvent this limitation by transferring literally dozens of embryos from a prize female to common brood stock females to carry to term. The potential implications for humankind and eugenics are mind boggling.

One should not think these approaches altogether new to human society. A woman who was having difficulty getting pregnant by her husband could always discreetly take another man to her bed. Conversely, in the Bible, when Rachel is unable to bear Jacob children, she offers him her maid: "Here is my maid Bilhah; go in to her, that she may bear upon my knees and even I may have children through her" (Genesis 30:1–3). What is altogether new is the technology with its awesome array of possible combinations. Resolution of the resulting moral, ethical, legal, and social dilemmas lags woefully behind the technology.

As many couples have learned, reproductive technology in its current state can be exorbitantly expensive and is not limitless. One cycle, one month, of in vitro fertilization costs $5,000 to $8,000. Going through the series of surgical procedures and waiting to see if pregnancy results is an emotional roller coaster. In spite of the emotional and financial burden, in vitro fertilization carries a relatively low success rate; there is only about a 25 percent chance of pregnancy. After four or five cycles, the success rate falls off, so clinicians often limit the total number of times a couple may try. Due to the increased risks involved with pregnancy in later years, many clinics will not accept women in their forties.

People are not only up against the biological and technological clocks. By the time a couple discovers their only option is to adopt, it may be too late. When they go to adoption agencies, they discover five-year waiting lists and an unwillingness on the part of most agencies to place children with people over forty. In short, couples who find themselves having difficulty getting pregnant usually encounter uncertainty, a confusing array of options, and not enough time.

"Will you see a couple for me?" asked an obstetrician colleague of mine who specialized in infertility. She explained that the couple had been trying to get pregnant for a year and a half. An infertility workup had been completely negative, which placed the couple in a small minority of couples (only about 10 percent) found to be "normal" at the end of an infertility workup; that is, no abnormality was detected. Ironically, such results put a couple at greater risk to have difficulty coping with their problem. The inconclusive workup creates a limbo that can foster considerable denial: high hopes of still becoming pregnant, which mask deep-seated fears that something is wrong that could not be detected.

Unlike many people the obstetrician saw, the couple still had time, because the two were in their early thirties. But she felt they were too tense, too wound up. She described them as Type A personalities whose reaction to their difficulty had been, "We're going to be able to overcome this. Everything will be fine." The obstetrician thought they needed to relax and come to terms with how they really felt about their predicament both to maximize their chances of getting pregnant and to be able to deal with reality, when the time came, if they had to make some difficult decisions.

When I first met them, Nancy and Bill were full of energy and enthusiasm, which I found somewhat incongruous with their reason for seeing me. Both in marketing, they were dressed in conservative business attire.

Once we were seated, I asked them how they were feeling about their difficulty getting pregnant.

"We're pretty relieved they found nothing wrong," said Bill, referring to the infertility workup.

"We're trying harder than ever to get pregnant," said Nancy, "It's probably going to be all right."

"How did you find all the tests?" I asked.

I knew Nancy had been through a grueling battery, which included pelvic exams, blood tests, cultures, ultrasound, X rays, biopsies, and even abdominal surgery to examine her reproductive tract.

"It was okay," she said uncomplaining. "The doctors and nurses, everyone, were great."

I appreciated Nancy's undaunted spirit while wondering if this was all she felt. Although physically much less invasive, Bill's workup too would have been emotionally draining: masturbating samples for sperm counts and waiting anxiously for the results, wondering if his ejaculate would measure up.

"I sweated bullets producing those samples," said Bill, jocularly. "But everything turned out fine."

As I probed the couple's emotions, I was hardly able to get past this untroubled veneer. Indeed, only one crack emerged: Apparently Nancy was having difficulty enjoying free time. Always hardworking, she was, over the last year, increasingly ill at ease whenever she tried to relax. Could they give me some specific examples, I asked.

"I have a difficult time on weekends," said Nancy, "I

don't seem to be able to enjoy quiet time. I used to have hobbies, but I can't enjoy them any more. Basically, I go in to work unless I have a very busy social schedule."

"Nancy hasn't been willing to take a vacation," Bill reported. "She's felt too driven and restless. In fact, we've planned a long weekend in Maine in just a few weeks. Although it will be the first time we've been away in over a year, Nancy still has mixed feelings. I've really pushed for it. Is that a bad idea?"

Before I could answer, Nancy reassured Bill, "I'm going to be fine. Don't worry. I'm looking forward to Maine."

I encouraged the couple to go away for the weekend, thinking to myself that it was good timing for our work. Nancy might be fine. But if not, the trip could shed light on the problems she was having with leisure time.

In fact, the trip was a disaster. After driving several hours up the Maine coast, finding the guest house, and unpacking, the couple went down to the beach.

"There we had this beautiful, warm, sunny day," said Nancy. "The beach was gorgeous, the water sparkling, and I started to panic."

"To panic?"

"I was okay for about an hour but then I began to have this lump in my throat. I went swimming again, sunbathed, and tried reading a book to distract me but nothing worked. Eventually, we had to leave the beach, and I burst into tears."

"Do you have any idea what upset you?"

"None. It all happens so fast. A panic comes over me. I simply can't relax. Now that I'm back on the job again, I feel fine."

I suspected relaxing caused thoughts and feelings that Nancy was uncomfortable with to flood in on her. Staying busy kept things at bay. Although Nancy was now feeling much better, the couple was shaken by what had happened. The couple's concern over Nancy's difficulty relaxing became the motivation in therapy. While much of the time the two remained upbeat, slowly more negative themes emerged.

The first of these was pressure from family and friends, many of whom recently had had children or become pregnant. "When are you going to be next?" was a refrain Nancy and Bill heard often. Two of Bill's brothers already had children; neither of Nancy's did. On the subject of becoming grandparents, Nancy's parents recently hinted by saying, "We're ready."

Like many people in Nancy and Bill's position, they had told no one of their difficulty and, therefore, felt quite alone.

"What would we tell people anyway?" said Nancy defensively. "We had all the tests and nothing was wrong."

"It's true the tests were negative," I said gently, "but the fact that you had to have them. . . . Everything's not all right."

Nancy looked at me soberly.

The next theme to come up was the issue of control, a common one in such situations. Nancy and Bill acknowledged this was the first obstacle in their lives that they had not been able to overcome by sheer force of will and effort. Both of them came from relatively protected, middle-class backgrounds. Under pressure to achieve, they had always done well.

"On the whole, life's been pretty good to me," said Bill, "but I've had to overcome some obstacles. I wasn't the best student in the world. That meant I had to be more determined and work twice as hard as some others."

"We came to feel," Nancy concurred, "we could accomplish anything if we set our minds to it. That is, so long as we had some talent and were willing to put in a lot of effort. Having difficulty getting pregnant is the first real obstacle we've encountered."

Unfortunately, while Nancy and Bill did well in situations ripe with opportunity and competition, this background left them ill-prepared for the kind of challenge they were now facing. While productive in other spheres, their upbeat discipline and control were the antithesis of what was called for here: the capacity to face limitations with emotional frankness and to take a more relaxed, passive stance.

After a few months in therapy, Nancy and Bill reached another depth, "admitting" they envied other people's children. "After Nancy had her laparoscopy," said Bill, referring to the surgery which was part of her infertility workup, "she had to stay overnight in the hospital. I slept on a cot in the room with her. You know where they put us? On the maternity ward."

"Unfortunately, that's standard practice," I said, shaking my head.

"Yes. We found out later. There's only one OB/GYN floor. But being around all those babies and their smiling parents . . . ," said Bill, a little choked up, "was really difficult."

I asked Bill if he could say anything more about his feelings, but he shook his head stoically.

"You become acutely aware of all the playgrounds in the neighborhood," said Nancy on the subject. "I never realized how many children's stores, maternity shops, and toy departments there are."

One week Bill came in with an observation. "I guess because of our discussions, I noticed something for the first time. On Saturday and Sunday mornings, I go out to buy the newspaper. This past weekend I noticed I've been using a different route on Saturdays. It took me a while to figure out why: The usual, more direct way, takes me past a baseball diamond. On Saturday mornings it's full of fathers and sons practicing. I don't know when I started, unconsciously, to go out of my way to avoid it. Now I realize why, because driving by had become difficult for me."

Slowly, the couple and I were getting a better sense of the pain and disruption in their lives. However, I felt they were not quite convinced. They remained fairly defended until we discussed the impact of their difficulty on their sex life. Here, we uncovered tangible proof of their tension and disorganization.

Characteristically, the couple opened the discussion with something positive. Said Bill, "When Nancy first went off the Pill, it had a wonderful effect on our sex life. We'd removed the obstacle to conception; sex wasn't just for pleasure any more. Making love was enhanced by this magical quality: The idea one of my sperm and her eggs would combine to create a whole new life, a synthesis of the two of us."

Picking up on this theme, Nancy related, "Sometimes after we made love I would lie in bed and wonder if it was happening, if some twinge I felt was that union. The rational side of me knew this was ridiculous but you get caught up in a kind of fecund fantasy life."

When pregnancy proved elusive, this early, joyous interlude faded. Anxiety took its place in the bedroom.

"Gradually sex became more mechanical," Bill acknowledged. "You feel more anxious and pragmatic. You just want it to work."

Most couples having difficulty getting pregnant eventually come to feel this way.

"At times sex has become a chore." Nancy went a step further. "We try to have sex as much as possible at peak times of the month. In the off times, one becomes almost disinterested."

"How often at peak times?" I asked, knowing many couples overextend themselves.

"At least once, maybe twice, a day," said Nancy. "Sometimes we even rendezvous at lunchtime. Oh, I can tell you exactly how often we've tried."

Reaching down, Nancy lifted her oversize bag from the floor and pulled out a sheaf of paper.

"When it comes to our sex life, these tell it all," she said, thrusting the worn and crumpled pages in my direction.

I did a double take when I realized they were temperature charts: Nancy's monthly cycle plotted for over a year.

"You're still doing temperature charts?" I expressed surprise. Couples are usually advised to do charts for only a few months.

"Of course," said Nancy, taken aback.

I stared at the lifeless stack of paper: The institutional green grids with their rough pen-and-ink graphs. The familiar biphasic curves with their midcycle temperature spikes signaling ovulation. Circles for the temperature readings. An X for every time the couple made love in the last year! Sure enough, in the middle of each month was a dense cluster of X's, sometimes more than one a day, indicating the couple's compulsive sexual activity. Then, on a few pages I noticed something that perplexed me.

"What are these?" I asked. "These dots over some of the X's?"

"Oh," Nancy seemed to panic. "Those were . . . shall we say . . . false starts?" She turned anxiously to Bill who had reddened.

"False starts?" I inquired.

"Well . . . ," Nancy seemed unsure how to proceed.

"Let me tell you how it all began, okay?" Bill finally said. "Do you have last October's score sheet there?"

"Yes. Here it is."

In the middle of October's graph, several days were marked "Phoenix." That month, Bill explained, he had to be away on business when Nancy was due to ovulate, the peak time of month for her to get pregnant. So, Nancy flew out to Phoenix to be with him for a few days. This was obviously a "big deal" said Bill, "with a lot of buildup."

"I was already stressed out by my work. The trip was proving a difficult one. Now Nancy had flown all the way out to sleep with me. With all that pressure . . . ," Bill stammered, "I couldn't get it up. I was mortified. Nothing like that had ever happened before. Thankfully, the problem wasn't constant, it came and went over those few days. But, it's continued to come and go since.

"When we got back to Boston, one of my buddies at work said of Nancy's joining me, 'You guys are the most devoted couple I know. How romantic.' If only he knew how thoroughly unromantic it was, trying to service Nancy in an anonymous hotel room."

Bill looked disheartened. Fortunately, I was able to reassure him. "Your problem is actually not uncommon. Many men under pressure trying to get pregnant will experience transient sexual dysfunction."

"They do?" said Bill.

"Absolutely. Sexual difficulties in your circumstances are viewed quite differently from problems arising at other times."

The two went on to explain that while deeply embarrassed, they did not think Bill's problem contributed to their difficulty in getting pregnant, because he was able to function most of the time.

"That's true from a physiological point of view," I responded. "But on a psychological level, surely this is an indication of the stresses you've been under and the toll it's taken."

Their guard now down, the couple had a heartfelt exchange for the first time since we began meeting.

"I have to admit," Bill expressed to Nancy, "at times I've resented how facile you can be about sex in the middle of the month and how disinterested at other times."

"Facile?" asked Nancy.

"Your sex drive's always been very sensitive to your mood and what happened on a particular day. I've been the one more consistently interested. Typically, you've needed a lot of foreplay to be receptive, and I've always been happy to provide that. Now, since we've been trying to get pregnant, it's almost the reverse. When you know it's a peak time, you're ready and waiting for me almost immediately. That's left me wondering why it hasn't always been like that . . . while at the same time resenting being treated like a stud service."

"I thought that would make it easier for you," Nancy responded. "I am quickly aroused in the middle of the month. I really want to get pregnant."

The two were now genuinely talking about how their difficulties had affected them. Here they were specifically discussing the gulf that had developed between them sexually with their respective roles in trying to get pregnant.

From her side, Nancy told Bill, "Imagine how I felt in Phoenix, when I'd flown all the way to be with you at this crucial time and you couldn't get an erection. I'd had surgery a few months before as part of this effort. . . . I tried to hide my disappointment from you."

Bill was taking this in when Nancy added, "If it will make you feel any better, I've had my problems, too. I don't have an orgasm all the time anymore."

"You don't?"

"No. I'm too tense. I don't enjoy sex as much as I used to. I didn't tell you because I didn't want you to think that was your responsibility because it's not. It's just the situation."

In their circumstances Nancy's problem was also common, I explained.

"I'm sorry," said Bill, emotionally, "but you know, it's still easier for you, Nancy. You can be completely competent while passive. You don't have to reach orgasm for us to conceive. I, on the other hand . . . every time that temperature chart's about to rise, I'm supposed to be able to perform on demand."

As a commentary on their situation, Nancy said, "You hear religious types say contraception demeans sex; that removing the possibility of procreation reduces it to a base level. My experience has been completely the opposite, which I never expected. It's been trying to get pregnant that has reduced sex to the most mundane, animal level."

"And then, for all our efforts, we haven't succeeded," said Bill heavily.

"One of the most difficult things for me," said Nancy, "has been adjusting to the shock. Perhaps it was naive, but I was quite unprepared for this. From the time I became sexually active, I learned about and tried many different kinds of contraception. My whole mind-set when I thought of sex and pregnancy was, *Prevent it.* When I think of the anxiety I

had years ago, the few times my period was a day late . . . ,"
Nancy shook her head tearfully. "After all the years trying
to avoid pregnancy, who would have ever thought it would
be difficult to get pregnant?"

Bill reached over to embrace Nancy. Their emotional
conversation had been a breakthrough. The three of us sat
quietly for some time with Nancy and Bill comforting one
another. Only after they both recovered did we return to a
few practical details.

I explained temperature charts were only meant to be
done for a few months. They are used to establish the pattern of a woman's cycle and to time specific tests during an
infertility workup. Continuing to chart Nancy's cycle indefinitely was a setup for the kind of pressure the couple had
succumbed to.

"We may have been told we could stop charting,"
Nancy tried to recall, "but, if so, it was said casually, not
like we were supposed to. I just assumed it would be better,
more precise, if we continued. It never occurred to me there
might be a down side."

In addition, Nancy and Bill were having sex more than
is usually advised. The standard recommendation is every
thirty-six to forty-eight hours at the peak time of month.
Twenty-four to forty-eight hours is the optimal amount of
time for a man to replenish the supply of his ejaculate. Since
sperm can remain viable in the vagina for up to two days,
there is no need to have sex more often. Having intercourse
more than once a day can even lower a man's sperm count.

"Every other day?" asked Bill. "We assumed the more
the better."

"On a purely physiological basis that's not true," I
responded. "When you add the psychological dimension:
What's the point of pushing yourself only to be unable?"

Nancy and Bill were not the first couple to make these assumptions and be overzealous. I suggested they completely abandon the charting and infuse pleasure back into their sex life.

"So we should have sex every other night?" Bill asked.

"No more 'shoulds' at all. Complete freedom and spontaneity. What you've been doing simply hasn't worked. It's been counterproductive."

"I'll still be charting my cycle in my head," said Nancy, a touch defiantly.

"Yes, but try to minimize that. If you know roughly when the peak time is, in a relaxed fashion just seduce Bill or let him seduce you. Don't throw down the gauntlet: 'Now's the time.'"

The couple laughed and said, "That's what it's often amounted to."

The next week Nancy and Bill were visibly more relaxed. They reported that pleasure and spontaneity were coming back into their sex life. Nancy was not due to ovulate again for "roughly a few weeks," they were careful to be vague in saying. This would be "the real test." A month later they reported all was still going well.

This turning point brought about a distinct change in our work. I had convinced the couple of the strain they were under and at the same time suggested relief. As a result, they had broken through an emotional barrier and in the process I had gained their trust.

Over the next few months, we progressed more rapidly. At one point Nancy said while things had improved, she was still having difficulty relaxing. Discussing the subject this time, she was more self-aware. Nancy said she viewed relaxing as wasting time. "I feel like I should stay busy.

Maybe it's to make up for not getting pregnant. If I don't have a baby, my career's going to be all the more important to me."

"Can you give me some specific examples of things you find hard to do in leisure time," I asked.

"What is one supposed to do?" Nancy responded, a little sarcastically. "Sit and have tea? Read? Do projects around the house?"

"Which you can't enjoy because. . . ."

"I don't know," said Nancy. "They feel like the opposite of being at work. At work I have a distinct itinerary, an agenda. I go from meeting to meeting. People come to me to solve problems and for support. My ideas generate work for others. I feel. . . more important."

"More important."

"Yes, like leisure is. . . ." Nancy veered away from her train of thought, most likely as a defense. "I know it's reached an absurd point. I ought to be able to enjoy a weekend. I used to."

Bringing her back to where she strayed, I commented, "You were going to say why you felt more important at work."

"Well. . . ," Nancy hesitated. "The other stuff, around the house, just seems too . . . domestic."

"Too domestic?"

"Too domestic, womanly, old-fashioned. You know, too wifely. Too much like. . . . Oh, maybe that's it: Too much like my mother."

This opened up a new line of discussion. Whereas her mother had been a housewife, Nancy was in a fast-track career. For some time she had been "running the other way" from her mother's attachment to home and hearth. The idea of having a baby flew in the face of that running.

"When I initially thought of having a baby, I had a lot of conflicting emotions. My first thought was to take time off."

"To take time off?" Bill expressed surprise.

"I never even mentioned it, I was so confused. I didn't think you would want me to. Besides, taking time off has become alien to the culture I work in."

Nancy recalled a few years earlier when a senior woman in her company became pregnant, "She had it made; her job was unassailable. I thought for sure she would take six months to a year off and set a precedent for the rest of us. Well, she had the baby and was back in less than three weeks!"

As a modern woman Nancy felt guilty wanting to take time off to be with a child. So, instead she talked herself out of these feelings. She resolved her original conflict by repressing one side of it.

"I convinced myself instead: This baby won't make me skip a beat."

"The baby hasn't even arrived," said Bill, "and we've already lost that battle. I don't know where you got the idea I wouldn't want you to take time off. It would be fine with me."

"A lot of my friends' husbands don't want them to take time off."

"Why not?"

"Because life is harder. We'd have less money, for a start," said Nancy.

"We can't have everything," Bill responded.

"That's what this is all about, really," Nancy said in an epiphany. "That's what not getting pregnant right away has made us confront, sooner rather than later: We can't have it all. There will be obstacles. We need to set our own priorities."

Part of the time we shifted our attention to Bill's issues. Also more emotionally aware, he acknowledged a sense of failure in not achieving pregnancy. He realized part of his motivation for having children was "to prove himself." While he "did not feel great" about this, he imagined most men felt similarly. Moreover, this was not the bulk of his motivation for wanting children. He sincerely wished to be a father, to see himself in his children, and to bring along the next generation.

A few weeks later when we focused again on Nancy, she said she had been thinking a lot about her job and the pressure she was under. In fact, she was considering taking time off while she tried to get pregnant. "Secretly, I think that's what I've wanted to do. I've come to that realization in the last few weeks, especially since knowing Bill would support it."

This was a significant change in Nancy's position, brought about by her soul-searching and the couple's improved communication. Not wanting to make such a decision lightly, they talked at length about it: between themselves, with me, and with their obstetrician.

As Nancy and Bill learned, the relationship between anxiety and difficulty in getting pregnant is complicated and still poorly understood. Emotional stress is known to influence a wide range of physiological and hormonal processes. In the extreme, anxiety can cause women to stop ovulating. Other, more subtle effects are also known. Stress, for example, can cause spasm of the fallopian tubes.

Clinicians walk a difficult line in this area. The question that inevitably arises is, Is the woman not getting pregnant because she is anxious? Or is she anxious because of not getting pregnant? What role might anxiety play? One does not want to burden the patient with any guilt or the false expectation that if she could just relax enough, she would become pregnant. One tries to give a couple a realistic appraisal of our limited knowledge in this area so they can make what is the best decision for themselves.

In their discussions with the obstetrician, Nancy and Bill talked about their future medical options. Nancy was surprised to hear that women undergoing in vitro fertilization and other high-tech means of conceiving often have to leave their jobs because of the physical and emotional strain.

"That did it for me," said Nancy in our next meeting. "I'm probably going to have to take time off anyway if we resort to that. Why wouldn't I take time off now? If I could possibly get pregnant without having to resort to the technology, obviously I'd far prefer to."

Nancy negotiated a four-month leave of absence from her work. She arranged to take June through September off in order to enjoy a long summer. To help her relax, Nancy and Bill rented a cottage on the beach, about an hour north of Boston. For the four-month period, Bill commuted into the city. Nancy came into town one afternoon a week because they wanted to continue their meetings with me.

In her first weeks free, Nancy tried to "make" herself relax. With time she took a less self-conscious approach and slowly "sank into the hot beach sand and accepted doing nothing." Over months one could see a remarkable transformation in her. One week, tanned and dressed in a straw hat, T-shirt, jeans, and sandals Nancy said jokingly, "I'm beginning to feel like a college student again."

At the end of the summer, Nancy returned to her job. She felt "better able to keep work in perspective." Since restoring her capacity to relax and enjoy free time, Nancy felt she could be more accepting if she did not become pregnant.

Then, less than a month after returning to work, she called one day overjoyed, "I'm pregnant!"

At our next meeting, she and Bill looked thrilled. They were trying to restrain their ebullience they said, but this was difficult to do.

"Why restrain yourselves?" I asked.

"Because we know about 20 percent of pregnancies are lost in the first few months. After what we've been through, we don't want to get too excited until we're past that critical period," said Nancy.

How they had changed I thought; now they were realists.

In fact, Nancy's pregnancy went remarkably smoothly. When they had a healthy baby girl she and Bill were elated. Afterward, the couple remained in touch with me periodically. In their late thirties they tried unsuccessfully to have a second child and remained somewhat regretful of postponing children for so long. This is another phenomenon one sees increasingly: Not only are many people struggling to have a first child but others find themselves unable to have a second or third. In view of our rapid social changes, current generations truly are an experiment. Perhaps future generations will effect a better balance between relationships, careers, childbearing, and family life.

TRAUMATIC JUXTAPOSITIONS

Richard and Sarah exuded anxiety when they first came to see me. A wiry, bearded man, one could tell Richard was not himself. He was solicitous of Sarah who looked shaken and strained. She had large, rheumy eyes that scrutinized me closely. She appeared wounded and fearful.

Richard went out of his way to pull two chairs together so he and Sarah could sit close to one another. With Richard taking the lead, the two explained how in the last few weeks their life had been turned on its head. Richard was an academic biologist. Sarah worked part-time for a nonprofit foundation. They had two daughters, aged eight and ten. The family was leading busy, productive lives until three weeks before when Sarah witnessed an assault between two men. She had not been herself since. Reaching over to hold Sarah's hand, Richard said, "The tense anxious woman you see here is not the person my wife usually is. Something's happened."

Sarah nodded in agreement.

I asked them if they could tell me in more detail about the assault Sarah witnessed. Sarah said she was on her way home from work when she stopped at a local convenience store. Shortly after she entered the shop, an ugly scuffle broke out between two men. What the men were fighting about was unclear but their violence quickly escalated.

"I was so unprepared," said Sarah, tremulously. "Suddenly, just a few feet from me, these two men were punching and grunting at one another. I can still see their fists swinging through the air. Blood streamed from their mouths and noses, covering their arms and clothing. I can almost hear the eerie sound of a crack when one of them punched the other in the face and broke his jaw."

I could feel Sarah's visceral discomfort as she described this distressing scene.

Like others in the store, Sarah froze watching the violence, "I was terrified."

She remained transfixed until police arrived and subdued the assailants.

"Most of us in the store were very shaken up. People were slow to leave and offered each other rides home."

Here Sarah stopped, as though unable to continue the narrative. Sensing her discomfort, Richard took up where she left off. "Sarah was unable to leave the shop, she was so upset. She wasn't hurt physically but she was badly shaken. I was called to pick her up and bring her home."

Once home, Richard and the couple's two daughters, Kate and Liz, did everything for Sarah. With this support she managed to get through dinner and the evening. But during the night she woke in a sweat from a nightmare of the incident in which she became a victim of the violence. She woke Richard for comfort and reassurance. Over the ensuing days she became increasingly anxious, had flashbacks of the incident, and her sleep continued to be interrupted by nightmares. Progressively, she was able to do less and less at home and work. Richard had to take over almost completely, driving the children everywhere and generally holding the family together.

In the past week Sarah had not gone to work at all. She had stretches in which she felt reasonably well and was able to do things around the house. But they were punctuated by periods of anxiety, tremulousness, flashbacks, and a fear of imminent danger. The fluctuations in Sarah's mood troubled and perplexed the couple. I reassured them that her symptoms were in fact characteristic of acute reactions to traumatic events. While Richard and Sarah agreed what she witnessed was traumatic, they did not understand the severity of her reaction. I suggested the incident might have tapped into a past trauma or brought to a head some current anxieties.

Sarah winced as I said this, responding that the latter might well be true. In the weeks before seeing the assault, she was under considerable pressure at work, planning a conference her foundation was sponsoring. Also, she was worried about her oldest daughter, Kate, who was scheduled for cosmetic surgery.

I inquired further, noticing Sarah's anxiety level rose sharply with mention of her daughter's surgery. When Kate was a year-and-a-half old, she had an accident which left a scar on her right shoulder. The doctors recommended Kate have plastic surgery when she turned ten, old enough to understand the procedure and cooperate with it but before adolescence with its self-consciousness about physical appearance. While the surgery was elective, had a low risk, and carried an excellent prognosis, Sarah was "beside herself" with anxiety over it. Trying to articulate her overwhelming fears, Sarah said: "Kate just seems too young to me to go under the knife . . . only ten years old. I can't reconcile myself to it."

Sarah's apprehension and her emphasis on "going under the knife" were disproportionate to the risk of the situation: exaggerating the vulnerability and emphasizing the violence and aggression of the surgery. There might be a connection, I thought, between the surgery and her reaction to the violence she witnessed.

Whatever the cause of Sarah's reaction, the couple was clear about the strain it placed on the family and marriage. Sarah was quick to say Richard had been wonderful. He was taking considerable time away from work to manage the household. However, his research was compromised and with Richard soon coming up for tenure, this worried them both. Sarah was still out of work. Kate's surgery was likely to be postponed given the family disarray. With all the stress and pressure, Sarah and Richard had been uncharacteristically irritable and short-tempered at times. They were anxious to see Sarah "back to normal" as quickly as possible, "before everything in their lives fell apart."

I had misgivings about this goal but refrained from expressing them. I prefer to see people uncover the source of their anxiety rather than opt for symptom relief. But with Sarah and Richard feeling so overwhelmed and vulnerable, what they needed now was reassurance. At a later date they might be encouraged to look deeper.

Fortunately, neither Sarah nor Richard were inclined toward medication as a cure. I rarely medicate patients on the first visit. I prefer to see what difference psychotherapy might make. Medications can always be added later. The difficulty with antianxiety medications is that they can introduce their own set of problems—tolerance, dependence, and addiction.

Just before the couple left, Richard added, "one more thing, I don't know if this relates or not. I hope it's appropriate to bring up. Sarah and I have always had a good sex life but since all this began, we haven't been able to have sex."

"It is important," I said, "and probably related to the trauma. Can you tell me what happens?"

"We used to be equally interested in sex and both took initiative," Richard responded. "Since the incident, Sarah hasn't expressed any interest and the few times I've made sexual overtures, she's been unresponsive."

Richard turned to Sarah for confirmation.

"It's true," she said. "I feel all tensed up and afraid. Not afraid of Richard but of sex. I can't explain it."

"I feel terrible that I've made any advances," Richard apologized.

Sarah interjected tearfully, "No, no. You haven't been aggressive at all. It's not your fault. It's me. I'm sorry."

As Sarah wiped her tears, Richard reached over and took her hand. The ordeal of Sarah's trauma had obviously been wrenching for both of them.

"I don't want you to blame yourself," said Richard. "That's the last thing I want. We just want you to feel better."

As time was running out, we only briefly discussed the abrupt change in the couple's sex life. Neither of them had any insight into why the change occurred. They never had sexual problems before. I suggested that under the circumstances, any sexual initiative be left up to Sarah, only if and when she felt ready.

At the end of the meeting I was left with a fragmentary picture of violence, fear, and anxiety. Why was Sarah not the person she used to be? How could one relate the assault she witnessed, her reaction to it, the pressures at work, her daughter's scar and pending surgery, the marital tensions, and her becoming averse to sexual contact? Which elements were most important? Was Sarah's anxiety the cumulative effect of all these influences? Or was one influence key? Was the basis for her anxiety, in fact, something she had not yet thought of or told me?

My intuition was that some as yet unknown trauma in Sarah's past would connect these disparate elements. The severity of her reaction to witnessing the assault and her subsequent aversion to sexuality suggested more was going on than simply a response to the current events. One sees this pattern—a severe reaction to a mild or moderate trauma—in people who have a history of earlier trauma, which is repressed but becomes dislodged by the fresh incident.

For the next several months my work with Sarah had a quality one sees with particularly vulnerable people. She came faithfully to our appointments and seemed quickly to become attached to the therapy. She was spontaneous in her speech and began telling me her history, chronologically. However, I noted she began with her college years, rather than her early family life. She alluded to "escaping" her childhood but refrained from going into detail.

Moreover, Sarah told me little about what was going on in her life outside therapy. It was as though our meetings had an existence unto themselves, somewhat apart from the rest of her life. People who are traumatized and feel vulnerable frequently compartmentalize in this way.

Finally, within the therapy, our discussions were more like monologues on Sarah's part. She rarely solicited my input and left little room for me to inquire. She seemed to want me to listen but in no way intrude.

All this I accepted, sensing Sarah needed this level of respect and restraint from me. I thought it best to follow her lead. Her slow, steady improvement signaled her instincts were good regarding what would benefit her.

One of the few things Sarah said of her childhood was, "From a young age I was an avid reader as a way of escaping my family life. Immersing myself in fiction allowed me to lead other people's lives rather than my own."

By junior high school, Sarah realized academic achievement could provide another form of escape: a ticket to an out-of-state school, a way to leave the family home. Early on she decided she would have to do extremely well and get into an excellent college to "justify" leaving her parents. She felt this particularly strongly, because she was an only child. Sarah also referred obliquely to alcoholism in the family.

Having grown up in Arizona, Sarah moved to Cambridge for college, which she said was "liberating." For the first time she felt valued by peers, and not just teachers, for her intellectual accomplishments. She also found herself considered pretty and attractive, another new experience for her. Her social life blossomed and she soon met Richard.

Sarah found Richard a "breath of fresh air." He was much more gregarious than she and introduced her to his wide range of friends and interests. For his part, Richard was drawn to Sarah's relative reserve. He felt solicitous and protective of her.

Richard also had a "fairly normal family," which was an important part of Sarah's attraction to him. He was one of four siblings in a close family that spent a lot of time together on holidays and vacations. Sarah felt Richard's family "welcomed her with open arms." They expressed delight that Richard, the scientist, had met such a sensitive woman in the liberal arts who would "round him out."

Richard was Sarah's first, and only, sexual partner. Their

sexual relationship, which developed in college, was another "revelation" for her. From the start, their sex life was very satisfying and a crucial part of their relationship. Sarah and Richard were married in the spring of their senior year of college and both went on to graduate school. He received a doctorate and then began his academic career. She earned a master's degree and became an administrator in a nonprofit organization.

Having children and establishing a family with Richard had been the high points of Sarah's life. She was quite conscious of creating "the kind of family life she would have wanted." They lived in a farmhouse in the countryside. Both Sarah and Richard's schedules were arranged so they spent a lot of time at home with the family.

As we talked, Sarah gradually improved. Although she continued to say little about her life outside the therapy, I inferred she was doing progressively better. She looked more and more relaxed in our meetings and made occasional references to things like Richard's no longer having to do everything around the house or visiting her work to discuss the possibility of going back.

At the end of the summer, three months into the therapy, Sarah took stock: Richard was working long hours, making up for the time lost when Sarah was "out of commission." She was planning to return to work in September. Her two daughters had thrived in summer camp. Kate's surgery was postponed for the time being. When I inquired into Sarah and Richard's sex life, she said, "There's been no change there."

While things were superficially getting back to normal, problems remained.

The week before Sarah started back to work, her anxiety level rose. In our meeting, she talked about the accident when Kate was a year and a half old. Sarah had just poured herself a mug of hot tea. In a flash, Kate reached up to the counter's edge and took hold of the mug. As she pulled it off the counter, she spilled the boiling water on her shoulder. The disfiguring scar was a lingering source of anxiety and guilt for Sarah. She regretted leaving the mug so close to the counter's edge, not anticipating Kate might reach up for it.

"It's something that's always made me question my mothering," said Sarah. "It's such a constant reminder . . . every time I dress her . . . when she wears summer clothes . . . in a bathing suit. . . ."

The brief rise in Sarah's anxiety level had prompted her to discuss this emotional incident from the past but her return to work the following week went surprisingly smoothly and she resumed the less emotional chronicle of her adult life. The only gradual change in the therapy was that she began to talk more and more about her daily life. However, she still avoided her childhood, rarely mentioned the assault, and remained uncomfortable with my offering much input or asking many questions.

The late fall and early winter holidays passed uneventfully for Sarah. Midwinter, Richard had a skiing accident, which left him on crutches for several weeks. Sarah coped well with the stress, managing the family affairs.

All in all, a year passed quickly. For much of the second half of the year, Sarah appeared to be functioning at the level she had been before the traumatic incident. While she seemed much less vulnerable, one could still see considerable sadness in her face. Although she was energetic, kind, good humored, and generous—a trooper really—beneath the surface one could see pain, suffering, and endurance. I knew these emotions had been etched into her face long before the trauma for which she came to see me.

On three occasions during the year I told Sarah that while pleased with her progress, I hoped one day we could probe deeper. Once was in response to a brief reference she made to her childhood. The other two times were when she alluded to the assault she witnessed.

"At some point," I said, "I hope we can discuss the assault in more detail."

Each time Sarah's eyes watered, she became more vulnerable looking, and said, "I know but I'm not ready yet."

"That's okay. Just so we're both aware."

Sarah nodded.

Much of therapy is waiting people out in one way or another. Waiting until they are ready to discuss the heart of the matter, meanwhile going with what they are comfortable with. Often the therapist is waiting for what is an unknown. You cannot say to an individual "We need to discuss X," because you do not know what "X" will turn out to be. In Sarah's case, there was something specific—witnessing the assault—that could be pointed to.

With Sarah I was walking a fine line. I was supportive of her symptomatic relief, her getting better and moving ahead with life. At the same time I did not want her to completely seal over whatever had been perturbed by the recent trauma. Were she to do this an opportunity would be lost. She would remain vulnerable to the same thing happening again, anytime, out of the blue. With my three brief comments during the year, in the most minimal way possible, I kept the door ajar.

"Anniversary reactions" are the emotions and behavior stirred up by the anniversary date of an important event. They are best known in relation to grief: the feelings a survivor has each year on the anniversary of someone's death.

But anniversary reactions can occur to a wide range of events or traumas. Often the first-year anniversary is the most powerful revisiting of the emotional landmark.

One day Sarah observed, "Next week it will be a year."

"One year?"

"Yes. Next Tuesday. May seventeenth."

The anniversary had not occurred to me, working as I was in an empathic mode, staying close to where Sarah was emotionally, rather than stepping outside the therapy, surveying the landscape for what lay ahead.

"That's the date, a year ago, you witnessed the assault?" I asked.

"Yes. I was on my way home from work. It was around three in the afternoon. Just outside town there's a little strip development. It's not in keeping with the old town; it dates to the 1950s. Anyway, there's a small grocery store in the middle of it. The shop used to have some character in spite of the setting, because a wonderful old man owned it. He retired and a chain took over. It doesn't have its former charm anymore, all spruced up and efficient. There's a fairly high turnover rate among the staff now. Still, it's convenient."

Did Sarah want to talk about the incident? She had gone somewhat afield describing the changes in the store's management.

"So it was late afternoon when you went in?" I asked cautiously.

"Yes. As I say, around three. I picked up one of those wire baskets you get in small shops and filled it with things. I was working my way up to the front of the store when I came to an open area with magazine racks."

Sarah went silent for a moment. She seemed anxious but prepared to continue.

"Is that where the men were?"

"By the magazines, just a few feet from me. That's why I felt trapped. . . that corner of the store is something of a cul-de-sac."

"I see."

"I learned much later that the men were working on a construction site. They had just gotten off work and were dirty and sweaty. They had bottles of soda they'd already opened and were eating cookies out of wrappers.

"I don't know what they were doing standing there. They were arguing about something. One of them shoved the other and that's how the fight started. Their soda bottles flew in the air. They fell to the ground punching one another, got back up, fell down again. I think I told you one of them broke the other's jaw. There was blood everywhere. They were out of control."

"Did anyone try to stop them?"

"No. No one in the store could have taken them on. That's why it lasted so long. The police had to come. They took them away handcuffed. One of the policemen is the nicest man. He often directs traffic in front of the kids' school. It was odd seeing him embroiled in something so brutal."

Sarah talked about the incident until the end of the session. As she left, I wondered if the breakthrough would continue.

Our next meeting was on the anniversary date itself. Sarah was upset and tearful. She had difficulty getting up in the morning and was unable to go to work. Richard and her daughters were aware and concerned about her condition. She was afraid of a significant setback, a repetition of what happened the year before.

"Last week, when I was describing the assault to you,"

said Sarah, "I couldn't believe how vivid it was. I've tried not to think about it for a year and there it was as though it had just happened."

I explained this is characteristic of traumatic memories. On the one hand they can be completely repressed. But if and when they return, even years later, they are extremely vivid with colors, shapes, and smells that are so evocative the person may feel they are reliving the experience.

"It gave me the chills to remember it so clearly. I hate violence. I've never been able to stand it on television, in films, or in books. I've gotten up and left movies. But I couldn't leave this time. It was real life, right in front of me, and I was trapped."

"Does that remind you of anything?" I asked. "Real life . . . violence . . . trapped?"

"No," Sarah shook her head. "It doesn't."

Was she conscious of then spontaneously beginning to talk about her childhood? Or was this an unconscious shift, another example of her compartmentalization?

"My mother was an alcoholic," Sarah said heavily, "a bad alcoholic. I think she probably always was, but it became much worse when we moved to Arizona. I was six years old when we moved for my father's job. We left Minnesota, which is where my mother's family lives.

"After the move, she really deteriorated, cut off from family, friends, and community. She was not outgoing like my father so she was unable to replace what she had left. In Phoenix, my father developed a social life—a whole new life—which my mother never joined him in. She deeply resented the move.

"Shortly after we arrived in Arizona, my mother began drinking more heavily during the day, every day. I remember her being smashed at my eighth birthday party, which was less than two years after the move. Some of the other children's mothers stayed around when they realized the condition she was in. They compensated for her, trying to hold the party together. I suppose they might also have been worried about their children's safety. My mother put six candles in my cake . . . she was so out of it, she didn't know my age. One of the other mothers had to add two."

Sarah's eyes welled up describing this poignant scene, but she held back tears.

For the next several weeks her anxiety level remained higher than it had been in months. However, she continued to work and did not have the major setback she feared. In therapy Sarah continued to describe her early family life, saying her mother's drinking was extremely difficult to discuss.

"No one knows," she said. "I've never talked to anyone about it before."

"Not even Richard?"

"Very little. When we married I made the final break with my parents. I see them infrequently now. My mother still drinks and I can't bear to be around her. It's suited both Richard and I never to discuss it. He's wonderful except when it comes to emotional issues. If things become emotional, you can see him get a little panicky and helpless looking, like he doesn't know what to do."

In one session I asked Sarah if her mother was ever abusive, because abuse is common in alcoholic families.

Sarah turned crimson. She said this subject was particularly upsetting. She felt guilty betraying family secrets, but yes, her mother was verbally abusive when she was drunk, bitterly sarcastic and critical of Sarah on a regular basis. "Nothing was ever good enough: the way I did things, how

I cleaned up my room, the way I looked, my personality. After we moved, my father gradually became a workaholic. Now I tell myself it was because my mother was drinking and he didn't want to come home. Maybe she was drinking because he forced the move on her and then absented himself from the family, I don't know. But the worst criticism she used to level at me . . . the one that hurt the most . . . was when she'd say my father stayed away because I wasn't a good enough daughter."

Here Sarah broke down into tears. We were reaching into deeply painful material. In another session, when I felt Sarah was ready, I inquired, "Was your mother ever physically abusive?"

Sarah stared gloomily at the floor for several minutes before she answered, "Occasionally."

I waited quietly until Sarah volunteered, "Very rarely when she was drunk she'd beat me senseless for some minor infraction. The worst time was once when I tried to escape a beating. She was enraged and crashed over a bookcase, pinning me down. Then she kicked the hell out of me."

Tears in her eyes, Sarah looked extremely sad and vulnerable. She was describing low points, some of the most anguished moments in her life. Listening to and supporting someone who is describing abuse is one of the most difficult things to do as a therapist. The pain I had observed some time ago in Sarah's face was becoming more explicable.

In a later meeting, after Sarah had described another beating, I asked, "Where was your father in all of this?"

"I asked myself that so often," said Sarah. "Remember I told you the time my mother crashed over the bookcase? My father came home; he saw my bruises and everything strewn all over the floor. He just quietly cleaned the mess up and said nothing. He was out of it, unwilling or unable to get involved. Was he in complete denial? If so, it was very self-serving."

"No one at school inquired of your bruises?"

"No. Not in those days. People weren't as aware."

Like most people with Sarah's background she was racked with guilt and self-doubt disclosing this history.

She said, "At a young age I figured out I shouldn't talk about what went on behind closed doors; my mother's drinking was something others should not know about. My father went to great lengths covering up for her on the rare occasions when we went out socially. My father and I never discussed my mother's drinking. Talking about it was taboo."

"You're breaking the taboo talking to me."

"Right. Sometimes it's hard for me to justify. I feel disloyal, like I don't have a right. Do I really need to tell you or anybody this? Was it really so bad? Am I exaggerating? Have I made things up?"

It is difficult to imagine the discomfort some people have divulging family secrets until one has sat with many such individuals over long periods of time. The taboo, secrecy, and resulting burden of guilt are the crowning blow in abusive families. The abuse not only has to be suffered but has to be suffered silently and alone. In my experience people almost always begin by underestimating and underreporting. This is borne out by their progressively remembering worse things and, when they get to a certain stage in the therapy, by corroboration from siblings, friends, or former neighbors.

In a similar vein, one day Sarah said, "I don't want your pity. When I tell you these things I don't want you to feel sorry for me."

People who have suffered silently and endured alone are so unused to sympathy that they often defend against it. They interpret all sympathy as pity, making them feel demeaned and vulnerable. This only changes slowly as therapy progresses.

Describing her childhood, Sarah began referring to another figure, her uncle John. Her mother's younger brother, he followed Sarah's mother to Arizona. Sarah described John as a "hanger on," a "down beat," and a "drifter." An alcoholic, he was part of the "extended family craziness" on her mother's side of the family.

"He was always very strange," Sarah remembered. "People say my grandmother spoiled him. He was her youngest and the most disturbed. There are stories from his childhood about his setting fires and harming small animals. In fact, once when I was with him he killed a kitten."

"Killed a kitten?"

"It was in Minnesota, before we moved. I was in my grandmother's backyard with him. I must have been four or five; John must have been twenty. A small kitten wandered into the yard. He picked it up by the scruff of the neck and started teasing it, pinching it hard and poking it with sticks. When the kitten became agitated, he started hitting it. There was a bird bath in the center of the yard. Eventually he went over and held the cat's head down in the water. I remember it's legs and tail sticking up in the air squirming as it drowned."

This insufferable scene had obviously been terrifying to a young girl.

"I froze," said Sarah. "I felt guilty not being able to rescue the cat but there was nothing I could do. John was so much bigger than I."

"Did you tell anyone what had happened?"

"No. Not in my family. . . . There was no one to confide in about those kinds of things."

"When your uncle moved to Arizona did he live with you?"

"No. He lived in boardinghouses or flophouses a town or two away. He'd be around for a while then disappear for months. But he always came back. He had this strange attachment to my mother. I haven't seen him in years. He eventually married and supposedly has cleaned up his act."

One day Sarah commented on how difficult it was recalling these grim memories. "This is so awful. I haven't thought of these things in years."

These memories were not exactly repressed; Sarah had ready recall of them. Rather, she had consciously chosen not to think about them for much of her adult life. Her stories certainly explained what she had escaped going off to college and marrying Richard. The question was: Was this all? Did Sarah's mother's abuse, her father's neglect, and exposure to people like her uncle John adequately account for her reaction to the assault a year before? Or was there more? Were there still worse, as yet repressed, memories?

The answer came two months after the anniversary date and shift in our work, when I found Sarah one day pale and shaking in the waiting room.

"What happened?" I asked as she entered the office.

After composing herself Sarah said she came into Cambridge early to do some errands and have lunch at a café in Harvard Square. The restaurant is one where patrons linger for hours, reading, writing, doing crossword puzzles, playing board games, or just people watching. Dramatic classical music is always playing in the background.

Sarah was sitting enjoying herself when, at the table

behind her, she overheard a mother criticizing her daughter.

"The mother was probably in her thirties and the girl about eight," Sarah began. "I noticed them when they entered the restaurant and sat down. Suddenly, I heard the mother say, 'Why won't you let me buy the dress with the lace for you? You look dumpy in the things you like.' The daughter protested awkwardly but I could tell she didn't know how to respond. 'You don't have good taste,' the mother, who was incredibly petty, continued. She kept at it, putting the girl down on a number of counts. I felt like turning around and saying, 'What are you doing? Don't you realize the effect you have on her?'" Sarah paused to catch her breath, then continued, "Children are so vulnerable. I thought to myself: As an adult that girl will end up in a psychiatrist's office. And you know what? She either won't remember what happened to her, the reason why she feels so low, or, if she has a vague memory, she'll question it and be full of self-doubt."

Clearly disturbed and agitated, Sarah said the scene reminded her of her own mother. Leaving no time to discuss this potent association, she plunged on, "Overhearing this tortured conversation completely changed my mood and feeling about the café. I sat staring at two men playing backgammon a few tables in front of me. They were very physical, muscular men in T-shirts. One of them had a small beer belly. I was watching them in profile, sitting opposite one another, hunched over a little table.

"I don't know why but I began to feel frightened. The men began disagreeing about something and gesturing. It wasn't a big argument . . . I don't know why I became so scared." Sarah paused, then asked, "You know how you take turns shaking the dice in backgammon?"

I nodded.

Looking embarrassed, Sarah said, "One of the men was shaking the dice, his hand close to his lap. Suddenly the rhythmic motion of his arm caused me to imagine he was masturbating. My head began to spin . . . the men in front of me . . . the mother and daughter behind me. . . ." Sarah looked ashen. With some urgency she asked, "Am I going crazy?"

Sexualizing the men's argument was certainly out of character for this normally decorous woman. However, it was not evidence that she was losing her mind.

"No," I said firmly and reassuringly. "You're not going crazy."

"What a disgusting thought . . . imagining the guy was masturbating. . . ."

"It's not disgusting. People often have those kinds of thoughts. For some reason, in your mind's eye, the scene suddenly became suffused with sexuality."

"I stared at them in a panic for a few minutes. They didn't notice me but others did. All of a sudden I was aware of people looking at me. I think I looked terribly scared. I got up abruptly, left, and made my way here."

"Do you still feel panicky?"

"No. I feel safe here. I just feel very odd."

"I'd like to continue to discuss what happened but I want you to let me know if you start to feel panicky again, if it becomes overwhelming."

"I'll let you know," Sarah said nodding.

"What just happened in the restaurant, does it remind you of anything?"

"Yes," said Sarah anxiously. "The fight I witnessed in the store."

"Can you elaborate on that?"

"The two men . . . in one instance there was a fight, in

the other just a disagreement over a board game. But the feeling was the same: the terror . . . feeling frozen . . . the sexuality."

"The sexuality?"

"Yes."

"In the store too?"

"I know. I don't know why I say that. I can picture the two men fighting, their ripped T-shirts, their sweaty look. . . ."

"What was sexual?"

"I don't know," said Sarah, concentrating intently. Then she said excitedly, "Oh, I see now. Remember I told you they were standing in front of a magazine rack?"

"Yes."

"They were standing in front of a display of dirty magazines. That was the background: a sea of cover girls. In fact, now I remember, they were fighting over a magazine." Sarah's excitement at recovering this detail suddenly dissolved into horror as yet new images intruded on her. "Oh no," she said, "I don't want to remember. . . ."

Drawing her legs up into a fetal position, Sarah began rocking, forward and backward, in her chair. Eventually she said, "I see another image of two men with a dirty magazine . . . my uncle John and a friend . . . in the basement of my house."

Knowing what Sarah told me of John and seeing her state, I knew this fragmentary memory was ominous. With tears streaming down her face, Sarah continued, "The two of them are dressed in paint-stained clothes . . . I don't know why. The scene has a suspended, timeless air. There's a thin stream of light coming through a crack. I have an image of his friend moving in a shadow. I have another image of John looking somewhat helpless. They've argued over something . . . I think it has to do with me."

An argument, John looking helpless, and his friend moving in a shadow: such fragments are the way traumatic memories often resurface.

Sarah and I sat a long time with her sobbing and me attempting to comfort her. For the time being she could not remember more but knew instinctively "something terrible" had happened. Fortunately we were able to run overtime so I could give Sarah as much time as she needed. Eventually, when she was composed, Sarah indicated she would like to go home.

"Shall I call Richard?" I asked.

"Yes, please do."

With Sarah so shaken and vulnerable, I had second thoughts. Based on previous experience, I said, "I need to ask you a question. I hope you won't be offended. It's important."

"What is it?" Sarah asked curiously.

"Often people who have been abused get into abusive relationships. . . ."

Sarah was shaking her head before I finished and said, "Never."

"He's completely safe?"

"Absolutely. He's been wonderful, patient, and gentle."

I nodded. "I'll call him."

For two weeks, Sarah required daily psychotherapy to support her through this extremely difficult period without hospitalizing her. I felt the intrusiveness of a hospitalization would be additionally traumatic. Gradually, over the two weeks, more pieces emerged until a full picture came together of what had happened. Along the way Sarah's anxiety and distress about the surfacing memories were compounded by a fear she would not be able to remember everything. Once the fragmentary memories emerged she wanted desperately to retrieve the full picture, which she was ultimately able to do.

Retrieving repressed memories, people are often helped by information from other sources. A turning point in the two weeks came when I suggested Sarah call her parents to inquire why her uncle John and a friend might have been at her home in paint-stained clothes. Having no idea of the context of Sarah's inquiry, her parents said, "Don't you remember he painted the house one summer? He had a friend, Eric, who helped him. You were around ten years old." Sarah subsequently recalled the two young men had been working on the house less than a week when she came upon them in the basement at the end of a day. She rounded a corner and suddenly found them drinking and pawing over a magazine. The two were startled but made no attempt to conceal what they were doing. Instead, Eric signaled to Sarah to come closer.

She remembered taking a few tentative steps, then freezing when she saw the magazine open to pictures of nude women. She thought the pictures bizarre and frightening. Shortly after she froze, Eric took a piece of cardboard and covered a nearby casement window. This created the ominous shadow and thin shaft of light in her original memory.

Sarah recalled her frozen terror as the two men began massaging their blue jeans and eventually exposed themselves. When Eric approached and began fondling Sarah, John and he got into a scuffle. John felt his friend was going too far and tried to stop him. Failing at this produced the helpless look on John's face. Eric prevailed, saying he was going to "finish what he started." Sarah recalled the unbearable pain, struggling to resist, being pinned, and the "horror of being pried open" against one's will.

As do many survivors of childhood rape, Sarah said tearfully, "I was so young I didn't even know what he was doing. I thought he must be going to the bathroom inside me."

The rape of a child has to be one of the most incomprehensible experiences. I find it one of the most difficult things to listen to, empathize with, and support a patient through. The pain and violation of reliving the ordeal are excruciating for the patient and therapist. At the same time it is cathartic and liberating for the patient to give voice to formerly silenced parts of herself.

As Sarah retrieved a complete picture of what happened to her, many previously inexplicable details fell into place. One could now understand the significance of her daughter Kate's surgery. The surgery was scheduled when Kate turned ten years old, the age at which Sarah was sexually assaulted. When a person has repressed events from her early life, the repression may become more difficult to sustain when her own children reach the same developmental age. Raising children entails a revisiting of one's own life, which challenges repression and denial.

Thus the sheer fact of Kate's turning ten had opened the lid on Sarah's repressed trauma, raising her anxiety level. In this context, the surgery felt more ominous and threatening than the reality of the situation. Her own childhood trauma vaguely stirred up, and, worried for her daughter turning the same age, Sarah transferred much of her inchoate anxiety onto the pending surgery.

In this already unstable atmosphere, Sarah witnessed the assault in the store. The crude fighting of the men gave her a sense of powerlessness and fear, which shook her repression at its roots. Her posttraumatic stress reaction was fundamentally a response to the dawning memories of her childhood sexual trauma. Her aversion to sexuality with her husband was now completely understandable.

In her first year of therapy, Sarah needed to keep both the recent and remote traumas at bay. During this time, she established a trusting relationship with me and, in the most minimal way possible, I gently encouraged her to probe deeper. Sarah's anniversary reaction provided the opportunity for her to take the initiative, going into the fearful material. The turning point came in the fateful session after Sarah fled the café. Overhearing the tension between the mother and daughter behind her and sexualizing the argument between the two men in front of her had opened the floodgate again, this time in the context of a supportive psychotherapy. Our discussion led to retrieval of the sexual context of the assault Sarah witnessed the year before. This finally opened the door on her childhood sexual assault. In that pivotal session the contemporary scenes juxtaposed with past events floated into Sarah's consciousness like disturbing pieces of a puzzle, which only reluctantly became clear in its agonizing image.

Retrieving the full memory of her sexual assault was just the beginning of Sarah's struggle. As is always the case, in the ensuing months she had to deal with a flood of anger and self-doubt. Why had she gone to the basement to see her uncle John, she asked accusingly. Sarah eventually answered: She was probably bored and listless upstairs; the presence of her uncle and friend painting the house was a novelty; perhaps she was escaping her intoxicated mother.

Why hadn't she left the scene immediately was Sarah's next question. She had trouble accepting that she might have been overwhelmed by fear and whatever she was feeling, whatever the reason she was there, could never diminish the men's crime.

Sarah thought she should have told her mother. But her mother was perpetually under the influence of alcohol. On many previous occasions her father had been disinterested. Moreover, Eric threatened retaliation if Sarah confided in anyone.

What did it mean, Sarah wondered, that she had repressed the trauma? It took her a long time to believe her unconscious must have felt this was her only option. Without someone to confide in, the conscious memory was unbearable. Sarah was deeply disturbed to think parts of her mind had been inaccessible to her for so long.

In another form of self-reproach, Sarah found it "revolting" she could have remained on speaking terms with her uncle. She "even went to his wedding," a fact she now found "reprehensible."

Gradually, Sarah's self-recrimination dissipated. Going over and over the incident slowly absolved her of guilt. As her guilt decreased, her anger rose. In addition to anger at the two men, she returned to the subject of her family background, the context in which the assault occurred and remained a secret.

Several more years of psychotherapy were required before Sarah reached a new equilibrium with her traumatic history. During part of this time she joined a support group of other women with similar experiences. This was another validating resource: to join other women speaking the unspeakable, to feel less alone, and to see others with the same experience who reacted in similar ways.

Initially the fallout from Sarah's discovery had a strong effect on her relationship with Richard. On several occasions I met with him individually, because in these situations spouses need considerable support too. I also met with them as a couple in the later stages of Sarah's therapy. Eventually, their sexual relationship was restored.

In the past few decades the field of psychiatry has done a turnaround on the issue of physical and sexual abuse in families. In Freud's day, abuse was regarded as too great a violation of social standards to be credible. Freud believed patients imagined sexual relationships with parents and other adults as an extension of their strong feelings toward them. Fortunately, in recent years strident patient advocates emerged within the profession to challenge such notions. Nowadays abuse is recognized as all too often true. A burgeoning literature and support network provide survivors with sanctuary for breaking the taboo and being heard and affirmed.

THE WOMAN WHO WANTED
TO SEDUCE HER FATHER

W hy can't I sleep with you?" Diana pleaded.
"It's out of the question," I said.
"Other people's therapists sleep with them. You read about it all the time in the newspaper."

"Yes, you read about it as a terrible transgression of the therapist-patient relationship. It's simply not going to happen."

Diana glowered at me, barely containing her frustration. She angrily swept her black curls off her face. Her pale blue eyes stared accusingly.

"You're a major disappointment to me," said Diana. "I feel like you're rejecting me."

"No," I responded. "Quite the opposite. I'm treating you with a lot of respect."

"Well . . . if we can't sleep together then I feel disgusting for having these feelings."

"As you know, I think the feelings are fine. Many people experience sexual feelings toward individuals they see in a position of power or authority to them. I suspect the feelings were an inevitability if we are to work things out for you so your relationships with men improve."

This idea had been a new one to Diana: sexualizing power imbalances. She would later call it the "first cut" in our understanding of her behavior.

Diana had been in therapy with me for six months. The sexual transference—strong sexual feelings toward me—had emerged about three weeks before. It was heralded by noticeable changes in her behavior and dress. She wore increasingly seductive outfits; cast long, lingering glances; and made ambiguous, suggestive statements.

I was relieved when Diana began to talk about her sexual feelings. Pent up they are more likely to be acted out and can do much more harm. They may be expressed indirectly in the therapy through irritability on the patient's part, which masks the sexual tension. Outside the therapy they may lead to friction with others or to careless sexual behavior. Once expressed, the feelings can be explored and validated while at the same time underscoring the boundary between the patient and therapist.

"I will consider it a defeat," Diana said shifting agitatedly in her chair, "if you don't agree to sleep with me."

"Hopefully," I responded, "you'll come to see it differently."

Diana's sexual transference was no surprise. She had a history of promiscuity dating to her adolescence. In one of the early weeks of the therapy she said, "I like to sleep with a man on the first date to get it over with. I can't stand the physical tension of waiting."

At the time I thought it might prove difficult for Diana to be in therapy with a man, because therapy necessitates a great deal of psychological intimacy. I was Diana's fourth therapist. The previous therapies, all with women, ended acrimoniously. In desperation, she finally sought therapy with a man because she thought "maybe that will work."

By her own description, Diana had a somewhat explosive, unstable personality. At times in the past she was preoccupied with finding out her diagnosis and extracted from therapists the label "borderline." This term connotes people who are prone to wide emotional swings, impulsiveness, and self-destructiveness; suffer from low self-esteem and lack continuity in their relationships or focus in their work; and are inclined to cast others in extremes of good and bad, forming intense, unstable attachments on the shifting sands of overidealizing one minute and devaluing the next. While diagnostic labels have some utility, I tend to eschew them, believing they pigeonhole people and make them feel worse about themselves rather than suggesting potential.

A few months before she came to see me, Diana had "disappeared" from a therapy that was going badly. The first year of that therapy had gone smoothly, a "honeymoon," but thereafter Diana "complained constantly" that the therapist was a bitter disappointment, frequently called the therapist at home between their appointments, and failed to pay her bill for long stretches of time. She needed a therapist who could "confront her crap," said Diana, with the remarkable clarity of people who have an awareness of their problem but feel powerless to change it.

In the month before Diana came to see me, three other therapists "declined" to work with her, saying they did not have time in their schedules after meeting once or twice. The therapists had been scared away, I thought. Diana would be a difficult patient. Besides her history of promiscuity, she also had periods of drug abuse. Her work and relationships had been "very unsatisfying."

In addition to many sexual relationships with peers, Diana had a prominent history of sexual involvements with teachers, professors, and employers. Also included in the list was a man who was once her lawyer, another who had done her taxes, and one who was her landlord. Some of Diana's affairs resulted from her being unable to say no to men. Others were the result of her seducing men in a position of power to her.

While Diana was very fond of men and "couldn't be without a relationship," at the same time she felt men generally took advantage of her. She had many bad experiences with men who exploited her vulnerability.

"Sometimes I've felt like a piece of meat," Diana said once.

All the same, she could not help repeating the experience. Struggling with her sexual transference, Diana and I traced her feelings back to her father with whom she had an emotionally incestuous relationship as a child. The term "emotionally incestuous," now gaining wider use, describes a highly charged, seductive atmosphere without frank sexual contact between the parent and child.

As a child, Diana was her father's unequivocal favorite. She received preferential treatment over not only her two sisters but also her mother. From the time Diana was very young, her father depended on her to be his companion and confidante. In return, her father spoiled her materially. Because they were not well off, her father's indulgent treatment of her was at the expense of the rest of the family.

Diana described her father as a "petty bureaucrat," a small-town official with an inflated view of his importance.

"I remember when I was eight," said Diana, "he was given an official car for his personal use. It was really quite modest, but a nicer car than most people in the town could afford. Also, its license plates had an official insignia. My father felt absolutely full of himself, all puffed up, driving around in that car. We used to go on Sunday drives together, just he and I, touring the countryside. He felt immensely self-important, and so did I sitting beside him, usually in a new frilly dress, my favorite doll in hand."

Diana's mother was not at all circumspect about her envy and awe of Diana's position. Her mother routinely asked Diana to lobby the father for things the mother wanted.

"He listens to you," her mother would say. "He'll do it if you ask him to."

At the same time, the mother could be severe in her criticism of Diana. Not infrequently she called Diana an "evil, scheming little girl."

"I was left with completely polarized perceptions of myself," said Diana. "From my father's side I walked on water and could do no wrong. From my mother's side I felt like evil incarnate."

However, said Diana, the real trauma was yet to come. When she reached puberty and adolescence her father broke with her. The earliest hint was when she had her first menstrual period. She recalled sitting in the kitchen talking with her mother about monthly cycles, reproduction, and other aspects of her coming of age. When her father entered the room and her mother told him Diana's important news, the father anxiously said he "never wanted that talked about in this house." He dispersed the mother and daughter, abruptly ending their discussion.

Although this had been troubling, Diana's relationship with her father was relatively unperturbed for another year or so, until she began dating. The first time a boy came to collect her for a date, her father was awkward and rude. Diana's preferential treatment from her father—the confidences, the Sundays idled away together, the indulgences—deteriorated. He began making unpleasant remarks about her "having grown up."

"I even tried for a while to forswear boyfriends once I realized what was going on," said Diana. "I wasn't ready to give up his affection that suddenly. But he turned on me. I went from being Daddy's little girl to a pariah."

Diana described one particular scene when she went on a date to the movies and for a soda with a boy.

"It was so innocent really," said Diana. "I don't think we even kissed good night."

But they arrived home a half hour past Diana's curfew. Both her parents were up waiting; her father was furious.

"While my mother looked on, he screamed at me for an hour, wanting to know what I'd been up to. I explained how innocent the evening had been but he wouldn't believe me. 'You better watch out,' he said. 'You're the type of girl people will be talking about. You'll disgrace us.' I couldn't reason with him. His mind was made up. He kept backing me into a corner, yelling at me."

"Did he threaten you physically?"

"No. He never lifted a finger to me in my life. But I felt powerless and humiliated. My father had simply lost all trust in me. He kept insisting the boy was a 'hot-blooded, virile young man' and 'more must have happened.' From then on he was always suspicious of me. It was awful. Of course, I had some growing sexual feelings so I thought maybe there was something wrong with me. Based on what my father said, I felt like a tramp. So . . . I became one."

With this deceptively simple statement Diana summed up a pattern one sometimes sees in people with a history of promiscuity. A parent, in Diana's case her father, is unable to deal with the child's adolescent maturation and treats the child's emerging adulthood and sexuality with disgust.

Diana's sexual acting out began shortly afterward. Her father's attitude toward her became a self-fulfilling prophecy. For Diana, the promiscuity served many needs. Ironically it preserved an unblemished image of her father who was "right" that she was "bad." In effect, she was being loyal to him by becoming what he said she was. At the same time, the sexual liaisons provided a substitute affection and numbing drug at a time of psychological and physical turmoil, grieving the loss of her father's affection.

One day, Diana said explicitly, "It was my father, figuratively speaking, I wanted to seduce all those years. I craved that special feeling I had with him . . . like driving around on those sunny Sunday afternoons in his foolish car." Here Diana laughed bitterly. "I never made the connection before between that and all the cars I screwed in during my adolescence."

If sexualizing power imbalances was the first cut in understanding Diana's relationships, this was the second: viewing her promiscuity as attempts to recapture her father. This was particularly true of the affairs with older men, authority figures, in her young adulthood. As this interpretation unfolded, Diana's sexualized transference diminished. She did, however, proposition me several more times and express frustration at my unwavering stance.

Eventually, I was able to point out to Diana that she resorted to propositioning me each time we reached a new limit of what she could tolerate emotionally and cognitively in our efforts to decipher her past. Within the therapy the sexual transference served the same purpose the promiscuity had in her life: a short circuit to avoid uncomfortable emotions. Gradually, the connection between Diana's relationship with her father and her sexual history became clear, the propositions stopped, and Diana began to express her appreciation for my refusal to take advantage of her.

"It's a new experience for me," she said.

A calm period in the therapy followed. Diana was in the midst of a career change. Since graduating from college she had done a hodgepodge of things, from waitressing tables to half-finishing a master's degree. Now she was working hard to establish herself in a free-lance career, writing music and movie reviews for a variety of regional and national periodicals. Overworked and underpaid, she nevertheless felt exhilarated about "building something" in her career after a "checkered" job history.

Diana talked frequently about the concerts and movies she reviewed. I found her unusually intelligent and well read. She was clearly very thorough in her work and original in her ideas. She was so inclined to put herself down, this might have come as a surprise had I not suspected she was an exceptionally capable woman.

The period of calm in the therapy was, however, relatively brief. Within a short while a new disruption occurred: Diana began calling me at home between sessions. The calls followed a distinct pattern. Diana would be distressed, usually tearful, about something that happened during the day. Looking for reassurance, she would not be satisfied with the comfort afforded by a limited phone contact. Each time she called I asked Diana if she wanted an extra appointment with me. She would go back and forth on this and eventually decline. The calls therefore had a tense, frustrating air. They came at all hours: dinner time, late at night, early Saturday mornings.

I knew from Diana's history that between-session phone calls were one of the ways she exhausted previous therapies. None of her earlier therapists had been able to set limits on her calls. Diana told me in one of our first meetings that her previous therapists were all "sucked in" to trying unsuccessfully to meet her needs.

In our meetings Diana and I made little progress discussing the phone calls. While experiencing them as frustrating, Diana could not articulate what her underlying motivation was. While I suspected a certain amount of anger and passive-aggressive hostility behind the phone calls, Diana would not agree. After about a month, I became concerned the calls were going to undermine our work. I felt they served no positive purpose. They needed to be curtailed before any resentment on my part contaminated the therapy.

In a gentle but firm way, one day I told Diana the calls needed to stop. Like all my patients, she knew my home phone number in case of an emergency. However, she needed to work on soothing herself when she was distressed and having a higher threshold for calling me. I cited her previous therapies, saying I valued her and working with her too much to let the situation get further out of hand. While she might resent my setting limits, my goal was to protect her therapy.

Instead of being angry Diana was "thrilled" with my position. I had "dared to confront her," whereas other therapists had not. She emphasized the confrontational aspects of my stance over the caring and supportive elements. She declared I was "wonderful," an "awesome" therapist. I thought this overreaction was characteristic of Diana who was inclined to see people in too good or too bad a light. However, the phone calls did stop.

Again we had a brief calm. Diana continued to develop her writing career. Several of her assignments were well received. Feeling good about her work and therapy, Diana began a new relationship with a local concert promoter whom she had interviewed for an article.

After dating Ron for about a month, Diana asked if she could bring him for a couples meetings. When I asked why, she said communication with Ron was not optimal. She thought there were problems in the relationship, but he was reluctant to discuss them. She had a difficult time knowing where he stood. He was somewhat self-absorbed and inarticulate about emotional issues.

However, when Ron came to therapy with Diana a few weeks later he was far from uncommunicative. Indeed, he unleashed a tirade of criticisms and resentments toward Diana who was stunned. He accused her of being moody and unpredictable, too flirtatious with other men, and lacking in confidence.

A guiding principle in couples therapy is to attempt to keep things balanced. I tried several times to give Diana an opportunity to respond, to enumerate her complementary concerns about Ron. However, she was too flustered to mount any response. She merely mumbled, a few times, something about his Jekyll and Hyde transformation.

The following week, Diana and I were scheduled to meet individually. The afternoon before our appointment she called and left a message in which she was quite upset. I was concerned because I thought she sounded groggy, her voice slightly slurred.

When I called her back, Diana's phone rang a long time before she finally answered. From her voice it was clear I had woken her from a deep sleep. Through her haze, she was hostile and defensive. Her life "was not worth living" she said, cryptically mentioning something about an overdose. In response to my many questions about what had happened, she would only answer lethargically, "It doesn't matter."

When Diana refused to tell me anything more, I told her I would have to send the police and an ambulance for her.

"Go to hell," Diana slurred, hanging up the phone.

I wondered why Diana was angry with me but had little time to speculate in the midst of what I thought was a crisis.

Diana was taken to the emergency room of a large, Boston trauma center. When I arrived I found her half-asleep and exhausted, propped up in a hospital bed. She had been given charcoal, magnesium citrate, and ipecac. In the vernacular, she had had her stomach pumped. In the end it turned out she only took a dozen mild sedatives, an overdose, certainly, but not potentially lethal.

Under such circumstances it is difficult to sort out the conflicting emotions in a patient's suicidal behavior. Still subdued and uncooperative, Diana insisted to the emergency room psychiatrist and me that she had not wanted to die. She felt desperate and suicidal when she took the pills but shortly thereafter had second thoughts. She tried to reach me but after leaving a message fell asleep.

Diana could give no explanation either for why she felt so desperate or why she later hung up on me. Especially troubling was that she had not known whether or not the dose she took could be lethal. She could have died even if she had not intended to. Her judgment had been poor, her behavior impulsive. Clearly her alliance with me was tenuous at the moment.

For these reasons the decision was made to transfer Diana to a psychiatric hospital to ensure her safety and assess further what was going on. Although unhappy about being hospitalized Diana had acquiesced and therefore was going voluntarily.

Diana wearily looked across her hospital bed at me. With tears welling in her eyes, she apologized for her behavior. In addition to looking remorseful I thought she looked afraid. At that moment a nurse entered saying Diana's ambulance had arrived. As I left the hospital, exiting through its frenetic emergency room lobby, I wondered why Diana had overdosed. Our last session had been the awkward couples meeting in which Ron unexpectedly laced into her. Had Diana been mortally embarrassed? Was she angry with me? Did she think I somehow facilitated Ron's tirade or was at least unable to stop it? Had she broken up with Ron in the intervening week? Why did she overdose the day before our scheduled appointment? In the emergency room, Diana had been too groggy and resistant to answer any of these questions.

I visited Diana's hospital ward late the next day. When I saw her, she looked much better than she had the night before. Since she had no roommates to bring things in to her, she had contacted Ron who went to her apartment and delivered a clean set of clothes.

The hospital staff told me Diana was being reasonable and cooperative. Based on their assessment, they thought Diana had been struggling with suicidal feelings, which transiently overwhelmed her at the time of her drug ingestion. However, they believed she had not really wanted to die. She was not thought to be an acute suicidal risk.

While this was reassuring, it was still worrisome that her self-destructive impulses could get the better of her, even briefly. Diana continued to be unforthcoming with any plausible explanation for why the overdose occurred. Without some handle on the circumstances surrounding suicidal behavior, one cannot feel assured anything is different or that it is safe to discharge the patient.

Diana and I briefly discussed the seriousness of what happened, even if she had not wanted to die. She now saw her impulsiveness and regretted the whole episode. She was upset over how disruptive the suicide attempt was and the "trouble" it caused others.

"I wouldn't do it again," said Diana contritely.

Suicide attempts are one of the most distressing things that can occur in life. However, in psychotherapy once one has happened, it is best treated as an opportunity: The chance to learn something important that the patient was unable to communicate directly. Weathering a suicide attempt always solidifies the alliance between patient and therapist.

"As important as your not wanting to do it again," I said to Diana, "is some understanding of why it happened. Presumably you were expressing something with your behavior that you felt you had no other way of communicating."

"I was upset," Diana responded. "I felt desperate."

"What were you upset over?"

"I'd rather not talk about it."

"Under ordinary circumstances," I responded, "that would be fine. We could wait until you were ready. I wouldn't push you. But this is different."

After a long silence Diana said hesitantly, "I was upset after our last meeting."

"Fair enough," I said encouraging her to go on.

"I was not looking forward to seeing you. I didn't want to discuss the couples meeting."

Diana went quiet again for several minutes.

"What were you upset about?"

Diana looked at me and shook her head.

"Was it because Ron was so critical of you?" I inquired.

"No."

What else might have disturbed her, I wondered.

"Whatever's on your mind is obviously difficult to talk about," I said, "but this is one of those instances when it's important to."

Diana looked away from me. A long, heavy silence followed. I waited her out. Finally, she began, "The meeting with Ron freaked me out. I hardly know what he or you said because I was so preoccupied with my own feelings. Almost from the minute we sat down, I felt this intense attraction to you. Ron looked really . . . unappealing. It was strange because I'm ordinarily extremely attracted to him. I was appalled to be having sexual feelings for my therapist and not the man I'm sleeping with, who was sitting right beside me."

Here was the sexual transference again. Diana had not mentioned it in a while.

"Have you been having sexual feelings toward me on and off all along?" I asked.

"No. They disappeared some time ago. I was taken completely by surprise. Now I know the feelings have a lot to do with my father, which only made it worse. Was it you I was attracted to or you as a father figure? I couldn't put it out of my mind all week. I've been so honest with you, I didn't know how I could come to my appointment and not tell you."

Diana said she thought she reacted in the couples meeting as though I were her father. Unconsciously she expected me to be cold, even hostile, with the introduction of Ron, as her father would have been. The sexual feelings toward me were an attempt to win me over, perhaps even at Ron's expense.

"I wasn't prepared for the strong feelings it would stir up in me," Diana explained, "to be in the same room with the two of you."

Diana said she knew her reaction was "completely at odds" with how I actually behaved in the meeting. "You were courteous to both Ron and me. You were obviously interested in helping us with our problems."

Discovering the connection between the sexual transference and Diana's overdose was a significant step forward. Her behavior now had a context in which it made some sense. However, Diana's explanation was essentially the same interpretation we arrived at before for the sexual transference. Given the force with which the feelings reemerged and her resulting overdosing, I felt there must be more; further depths to the sexual transference which we needed to explore. Of course, it would take a long time to uncover all the nuances of what had happened. Meanwhile, I was relieved we were back on track.

I was therefore surprised when I arrived to see Diana the next day to find her noticeably distressed. When I asked why, she said, "Because of our meeting yesterday."

"What about the meeting?"

"I don't want to be discussing those things with you now."

"What do you mean *now*?"

Diana raised her voice impatiently, "Now that we're stopping."

"Stopping?" I expressed my surprise.

"You're not going to continue to work with me, are you?"

"Of course I am. Why do you ask?"

Diana burst into tears. She seemed genuinely taken aback and confused.

"You're really going to stick by me through this?" she said, streaking her tears across her face.

"Absolutely. What made you doubt it?"

"Nothing you've said." Diana continued to cry. "It's just that . . . "

Once she collected herself, Diana said one of her former therapists had a "contract" with her that if she ever made a suicide attempt, the therapist would no longer work with her.

"She said if I did that it would mean our relationship was so poor I should work with someone else. I thought all therapists felt like that."

"No," I responded. "I don't. You needn't worry."

Diana said her fears were compounded by the hospital staff's "barraging" her with questions about our work: How she felt about it. Whether or not she thought the therapy was going well. Were she and I a good match?

"They seem to be looking for me to be critical," said Diana cautiously, as though she feared saying something that would disturb me.

"That's their job," I responded. "That's what they should be doing. Whenever something like this happens it's important to evaluate the treatment."

Diana said she felt "overwhelmed."

"Do you have any doubts about whether or not we should continue?" I asked.

"No. I just can't believe you'd stick with me."

"I want you to be open with the staff," I said, "about any reservations you have concerning our work and to also feel you could discuss them with me. It's crucial at this juncture, following your overdose."

"If I had reservations," said Diana, "I would tell you."

Diana's overdose and subsequent revelations opened up a wealth of material for us to work on. However, as prolonged hospitalization runs the risk of fostering dependence and regression, the short-term goal was to discharge her from the hospital. She was not acutely suicidal and those two early meetings following her overdose firmly reestablished our alliance. Following the second meeting, Diana was notably relieved and her condition continued to improve. By the end of the week the hospital staff believed that Diana was ready to leave.

One final piece of fallout from the hospitalization was Diana's parents' reactions.

"It's just like you to do something like this," her father said when she called them.

Her parents declined to come visit her.

"You wouldn't want us to see you in that condition," said her mother.

Her father urged her "not to leave the hospital in a hurry."

"You're very disturbed," he told Diana. "You shouldn't leave the hospital until you're all better."

"They haven't a clue what I'm dealing with," Diana reflected. "Imagine saying 'You wouldn't want us to see you in your condition' after I asked them to visit. My father says I'm very disturbed. There's no sense it might have anything to do with how he treated me. I'm tired of the manipulation." Recovering her sense of humor, Diana said jokingly, "If I waited until I was all better, I'd be here for years."

Once Diana was discharged from the hospital she and I maintained the momentum discussing the events leading up to her drug ingestion. It is not uncommon for symptoms—in this instance Diana's sexual transference and her overdose—to have multiple determinants. Sexual transferences themselves are not uncommon. Many people, in and out of therapy, develop sexual feelings toward individuals for reasons other than romance or pure physical attraction. What was unusual was Diana's overdose, which resulted from the combination of her character structure and the sexual feelings. Given this potentially lethal combination, I felt some urgency to get to the bottom of things.

In our first meeting after Diana left the hospital, we discussed the couples meeting which occurred before the overdose in detail. Diana emphasized how "receptive" I was to her and Ron. I was genial to both of them and interested in their relationship.

"You were doing what my father had never done," said Diana.

In spite of these positive feelings, she reacted on the basis of the quite contradictory expectation that I would behave more like her father. This was Diana's explanation for why the sexual transference emerged. She felt the sexual feelings were some combination of wanting to seduce me into being nice to the couple and/or joining with me if I were hostile to Ron.

"Remember," Diana commented, "I have absolutely no experience of ever sitting talking comfortably with my father and a boyfriend."

In another meeting, Diana and I discussed the week between the couples meeting and her overdose. Diana said she was "obsessed with the sexual feelings" that arose in the couples meeting.

"I couldn't put what happened out of my mind. It was like I was traumatized or something."

"Did you see Ron that week?"

"Yes."

"How did you feel toward him?"

"Alienated, because he didn't know anything about what was weighing on my mind. Guilty for having sexual feelings for someone other than him. Ashamed. Embarrassed. Confused."

"Did sexual feelings toward Ron come back in the days following the meeting?"

"No. They didn't until after you and I discussed it in the hospital. Once I talked about it I felt better and things began to improve with Ron."

In a later meeting Diana and I discussed the day of the overdose. She had worked at home all day but was unable to get anything done. She felt restless and agitated. The night before, Diana slept with Ron for the first time since the couples meeting. She felt "totally confused" sexually.

"I felt so uncomfortable, like there was no way out of this morass of feelings."

Diana tried to elaborate any other feelings she had that day but kept coming back to the same ones: guilt, embarrassment, confusion.

"Did you feel any anger?" I asked.

"At what?"

"Anything. Anger over being confused. Anger at Ron. Anger at me."

"No," said Diana. "I didn't feel any anger."

I thought Diana was defending against some of her feelings here. Whenever someone makes a suicide attempt one presumes the presence of significant anger, in addition to sadness and despair. In the context of therapy, suicidal behavior implies some anger at the therapist. The real source, or target, of the anger may be another figure, in Diana's case her father. Of course, she was sitting on substantial anger toward him given her experience. But if she were angry with him and feeling positively toward me, she would not have overdosed. The anger must have spilled over to include me for that to occur. This spillover was what we needed to elucidate.

At our next session I brought up the brief phone conversation between Diana and me on the day of her overdose. The call was the one time Diana was overtly hostile. She refused to tell me what had happened and eventually hung up on me. Diana said she could not recall being angry because she was so sedated during the conversation.

"Do you remember the call at all?" I asked.

"Yes. I remember you calling back and I know I hung up."

"Why did you hang up?"

Diana reached for another explanation. "I had already taken the overdose by then so I was reacting as though the therapy was over. I was assuming you would stop seeing me. If I was angry, that's probably why."

This was too elaborate an explanation, too self-conscious an idea, to have been operating under the influence of the sedatives. More likely, the sedatives were disinhibiting, removing Diana's defenses against expressing anger toward me, uncovering the hostility. However, she was too defended for me to push further just now.

While Diana and I were going over the events surrounding her overdose with a fine-toothed comb, she was at the same time reequilibrating the rest of her life. Because she was a free-lance writer, the hospitalization produced minimal disruption in her work.

A bigger adjustment was that Ron "exited the scene," as Diana put it. He broke up with her a month after her hospitalization. Although hurt, Diana said Ron's behavior did not surprise her. This was what she expected; it was typical of her experience with men.

Gradually, over the next month or two, Diana slowly began to express negative feelings toward me. Her characterization that I was steady and composed changed: Now I was remote; she did not think she knew me well enough. My insights into her behavior were no longer satisfactory: I had not provided enough of them; she was disappointed with me. I welcomed this development, thinking the feelings had been there for some time. The more Diana could express them, the less she would need to act them out.

One week Diana's complaints reached new heights. She was bogged down in her work, having difficulty finishing several articles. She felt she was doing poorly. She began halfheartedly by saying I was not working my "psychic wizardry" on her. Before long this escalated to her saying that I did not really care about her. I was cold, indifferent. I had been interested in her when she first came to see me. She thought at first I viewed her as a "project," someone I could "fix." But I was disappointed she had not just "taken off" and done well. I no longer felt like "being bothered" with her. She was a "burden."

Once or twice I tried to interject, to correct the perception that I did not care. Diana's response was to accuse me of being defensive. I decided to remain quiet. Her litany was so clearly transferential: the idea that I had lost interest in her, gone cold, like her father. Nothing I could say would help the situation just now. Sometimes it is better to simply listen, to wait for the storm to pass before trying to pick up the pieces.

The next week Diana said it "felt good to get so angry" with me. However, at the height of the anger she was once again overcome with wanting to seduce me. The sexual feelings toward me were, she said, "still running high." Linking her sexual feelings toward authority figures with anger, she said, "That's a far cry from wanting to win them over."

"Right," I responded, impressed with this connection.

Pursuing this further, I asked, "What became of your relationships with bosses, professors, other authority figures?"

"You mean once they became sexual?"

"Yes."

"Everything you can imagine," said Diana vaguely.

"Meaning?"

"Everything from one-night stands to lasting relationships."

"How long would they last?"

"Obviously not forever," Diana responded testily.

I pressed Diana to run through the relationships and calculate how long they survived. She spent a while doing this, half-aloud. In the end, the tally was dismal: After becoming sexual, none of the relationships lasted more than a month.

"What became of the jobs and courses?" I asked.

"I left the jobs," said Diana soberly. "I never finished the courses . . . the incomplete master's degree I told you about."

Diana and I sat staring at one another. The same inevitable conclusion came over both of us.

"All the relationships were destroyed by becoming sexual," said Diana breaking the silence. "I trashed them."

"So it seems," I responded.

"Sleep with me," Diana pleaded.

"No."

"I hate you."

"Good. That's progress."

"For me to hate you?"

"For you to be able to say it."

"I really do!"

"I know."

"Then again I don't. I know the hatred comes from deep

within me somewhere. I like you even though I hate you. I can feel the conflict."

"Good," I said resolutely. "That conflict is central to your struggle with men."

We now had a much better handle on the complexity of Diana's feelings toward men and authority figures in particular. Just a short time ago she had been heavily defended against her anger toward me. The anger had since broken through, and now she had connected it with her sexual feelings toward me. Through all of this she had managed to maintain some perspective on what was happening. This combination of emotional breakthroughs and self-awareness is ideal in psychotherapy.

The next week Diana unleashed another tirade against me. Among other things she "couldn't believe" our last meeting. The conclusions we reached were true but did I not realize she was unstable? Clearly alluding to her overdose she said, "I'm surprised you're not treating me with kid gloves after what happened."

Diana's tone was almost threatening. However, to treat her with kid gloves would be the worst thing I could do. My response to her anger and distress was to say sympathetically, "I think you're upset because we're getting to the bottom of things."

"You're not afraid of my anger, are you?" said Diana, her fury trailing off into exhaustion.

"No. I'm not."

"Everyone else has been."

"In fact, it's essential for us to go headlong into it. Otherwise it may overwhelm you again."

I knew Diana felt under pressure but I was not prepared for her announcement the next week.

"I'm leaving therapy."

"You are?"

"Therapy with you anyway. I have an appointment with someone new this Friday."

Diana reiterated her complaints. The solution, she decided, was to find a new therapist. I realized immediately things had become too heated for Diana. She was pulling back so I did likewise. She needed room, psychologically.

As we talked, it emerged Diana still wanted to keep her appointment with me the next week. I thought this strong evidence of her ambivalence. In spite of how resolutely she presented herself, I doubted her decision was firm. I gently told Diana I thought it would be a mistake for her to change therapists at this point but, of course, that was her choice. I was at least relieved she was not quitting therapy altogether. I hoped she worked these issues out with someone, if not me. Making my position clear, I left her plenty of space. Leaving things so open does require tolerating considerable uncertainty about the outcome.

The next week Diana looked mildly dejected. Of the new therapist she said, "He wouldn't touch me with a ten-foot pole. I told him about everything, including my suicide attempt."

Of course, she chose to tell him in whatever fashion she did, I thought, perhaps wanting to scare him away.

"I guess it's back to you and me."

"Why are you keeping me?" Diana inquired wearily.

This was an interesting reversal. Diana had just been talking about leaving me. Now she was asking why I did not let her go. I suppose the point at which she announced she was seeing another therapist would have been an opportunity to terminate with her, if that was what I wanted. Of course, it was not.

I answered Diana, "Because I care. I think you are a talented, capable woman. Your life should be going more smoothly than it is and I'd like to see you get there."

Diana responded flippantly, "How can you care if you won't sleep with me?"

"You mean, how could I sleep with you if I cared?"

In a stark moment of truth Diana said exasperated, "Why don't you just fire me?"

Diana's behavior throughout the therapy suddenly came together in a new way for me.

"That's what you've wanted all along, isn't it? Starting with the propositions, the phone calls at home, the overdose, the tirades, and now looking for another therapist. You don't know what to do with me."

"If you'd slept with me it would have all been over long ago."

"Exactly. A quick physical intimacy that would have destroyed everything else."

"You're the first man who's stuck by me and not taken advantage of me," Diana said, becoming overwhelmed. Through a wellspring of conflicted emotions she added, "It makes me feel . . . self-destructive."

"Self-destructive?" I said, taken aback by this final twist.

"I don't feel I deserve it. It makes me too uncomfortable. I feel like crawling out of my skin."

The following week I began by saying, "My treating you well makes you feel self-destructive."

"Yes. When you said you cared and that's why you hadn't gotten rid of me . . . that's how I felt, overwhelmed. Incredibly uncomfortable. Undeserving."

"And you sexualized those feelings."

Diana nodded, adding, "As usual, I asked you to sleep with me . . . the emotional short circuit, as you sometimes call it. I guess now I have more of a sense of what's in that circuit."

"It's not so short any more."

Diana smiled. The two of us sat silent. Not a pregnant pause but the kind of restful quiet that can only happen once certain barriers have been removed between people.

"Maybe the same thing happened in the meeting with Ron," Diana commented.

"How do you mean?"

"You were being very receptive and warm, not at all like what I expected based on my experience with my father. Maybe you were being nicer than I could stand. I had the same feeling in that meeting, of wanting to jump out of my skin. I couldn't face you the next week. That's when I overdosed."

This was the last, and perhaps most important, feeling underlying Diana's sexual tension and self-destructiveness in the therapy: the disorganizing influence of being treated well on people who are not accustomed to it. On the interpersonal level, this had prevented Diana from having healthy relationships. In the work sphere it barred her from a fruitful career. People whose self-esteem is terribly shoddy, who have internalized a negative self-image, will go about life repeating experiences that reinforce this entrenched self-view. They are trapped in this position by powerful self-sabotaging reflexes, which are triggered whenever things begin to go better for them.

As we talked about this over the next several weeks, Diana said she could now really feel the anger that had been there all along in the desire to seduce me.

"In wanting to seduce you, I wanted to pull you down," she said. "*Trashing* is really the right word for it."

"But you also trash yourself," I responded. "You trash your legitimate longings to be valued, nurtured, and treated well."

Diana and I reviewed, many times over, all the threads in her sexual transference: sexualizing the power imbalance between her and authority figures, wanting to win over father figures, and trashing them in the same breath, all the while trashing herself. It comes as a surprise to some people that virtually any emotion—anger, sadness, dependence, and insecurity, as well as warmth, caring, and tenderness—can be sexualized.

Diana's tolerance for being treated well gradually improved as her therapy progressed. Although the sexual transference did not reappear, there were other difficult stretches in her treatment. She went through a period of feeling dependent on the therapy and, therefore, me. This is not something to be encouraged in therapy but is at times a necessary transition. In a similar vein, Diana struggled periodically with acknowledging to herself how much she cared about the therapy without becoming self-destructive.

At times Diana and I strongly disagreed. I would have to confront her about ongoing, progressively milder, self-destructive behavior in relationships or her work. These confrontations continued to be tense for some time.

Many more stories emerged of Diana's psychological abuse in her family. The way in which as a child she was pitted by each parent against the other became increasingly distasteful as Diana fleshed it out. In spite of much soul-searching, however, she never felt she was physically or sexually abused. As was seen in the last chapter, recent advances in the field have provided a watershed for people who were physically or sexually abused. While this has been a positive development, it has sometimes made people without such a history feel left out in the cold. In my experience, as Diana's case illustrates, psychological abuse can often be crippling in its effect.

As a late development in Diana's therapy, she learned there was a history of incest in her father's family. Her mother told her this as a possible explanation for why her father reacted the way he did to her adolescence. He was perhaps fearful of a repetition when he suddenly distanced himself from her. He may have feared his own impulses could not otherwise be controlled.

While not diminishing her sadness and disappointment over what had happened, this revelation did allow Diana to feel some understanding and warmth toward her father. In this regard, Diana was one of the lucky ones: Few people learn such a detail, so crucial to understanding their experience.

A book on psychotherapy and sexuality would not have been complete without a discussion of sexual transferences. In recent years, many cases of sexual relationships between patients and therapists have been highly publicized in the media. Too often these liaisons begin with seductive therapists rather than seductive patients.

Sexual transferences are examples of the powerful emotional force fields both patients and therapists are subject to in psychotherapy. One should always be clear that managing those force fields, maintaining appropriate boundaries, is solely the responsibility of the therapist. When this is forgotten, transgressions occur.

AFTERWORD:
SEX AS METAPHOR

I have presented the material in this book as cases, rather than in a more didactic format, because case descriptions allow clinical work to speak for itself, in all its richness and complexity, relatively unfettered by jargon or theory.

As the book comes to a close, I would like to underscore one theme in particular. In the Introduction, I commented that again and again in psychotherapy, sexual issues and symptoms can be seen as metaphors for the larger psychological stresses and strains in an individual's life. Sex is such a powerful metaphor because it is a microcosm of interpersonal relationships. Sexuality embraces the full panoply of human emotions and behavior, yet expresses them in a condensed, elemental form. Viewed from this perspective, the sexual arena is a distillation, a shorthand, in which psychological motifs can often be seen more readily than they can in more complex social interactions.

Since the earliest days of psychotherapy, Freud made sexuality central; but for him, sex was literally rather than metaphorically so. According to Freud, it was the frustration of sexual drives encountering social constraints that produced psychic tension and, therefore, symptoms. This is still sometimes true; however, perhaps because we live in an era of far less constraint on sexual behavior, nowadays the opposite is more likely to be the case: Emotional distress— anger, sadness, disappointment, grief—arising in interpersonal relationships can become infused into sexuality, which then symbolically expresses the psychic tension. Sex imitates life, rather than the other way around.

Thus, a young man's pornography addiction is a ritual revisiting, a metaphorical expression, of the unresolved grief over his father's disappearance and death years before. A woman's difficulty reaching orgasm in the presence of a male partner proves to be the sexual manifestation of her more general power struggle with men. And another woman's overwhelming sexual transference is a many-layered metaphor for her hostile attachment, self-loathing, and conflictual desires to both have and destroy an elusive father figure.

In my experience, few patients actually report overt sexual symptoms at the outset of therapy. Only those specifically seeking treatment for a sexual problem do so; a man who cannot wear condoms or a couple who are unable to consummate their marriage. These are the exceptions, accounting for less than 10 percent of a general psychiatric practice.

More often, sexual problems are obscured in one fashion or another. Typically, people lead with more global symptoms: A man reports numbness while covering up a pornography addiction. A couple describe escalating arguments rather than premature ejaculation and anorgasmia. In some cases, people are not so much hiding sexual issues as they are unaware of their meaning and relevance (for example, promiscuity) until well into psychotherapy. And, of course, some sexual traumas are not reported because they are buried outside of conscious awareness and only emerge through introspection.

In general, most people are reticent about sex because they were taught early in life that sexual matters are extremely private. One patient told me that, as a young boy, at night he often heard his mother and her boyfriends engaged in sexual play (his parents were divorced). In his grandfather's workshop he stumbled upon boxes of pornographic magazines. "Even my grandmother," he said ruefully, "kept a stash of erotic novels in her desk drawer!" Yet when he came of age, his father awkwardly handed him a book on sex and made it clear he could not talk about it. "So I became incredibly curious about this powerful force all the adults around me seemed to be into but could not discuss. I learned sex was something secret, relegated to boxes, basements, closets, and drawers."

And so for most of us, sex is sequestered from the rest of life. In our open, self-conscious culture, we candidly discuss almost anything else in everyday conversation: relations with spouses, children, and parents; job aspirations and failures; our salaries; who we voted for; our physical, and even mental, health. Sex, that powerful river running through all, remains apart, rarely subject to scrutiny.

Yet, as we have seen, sex is central and always illuminating. People in psychotherapy gradually become at ease with and see the relevance of their sexual behavior, fears, fantasies, and dreams. Even where sexual symptoms are not the most prominent ones, sexuality is extremely useful for seeing psychological patterns. Hidden in the interstices of an eating disorder, for example, are sexual innuendoes that once again bespeak larger themes.

A few people are initially disappointed to discover the influence of psychological scars on their sexual behavior. Thinking sex a thing apart, they had hoped it would be unaffected. On the contrary, I suggest, one should expect sexuality to be one of the first areas to succumb to psychological influences. And so, I always view sexual material through this lens, mining its metaphorical meaning for psychological insights.